KATRINA
BEFORE & AFTER

SunHerald
SOUTH MISSISSIPPI'S NEWSPAPER

Editors: John Fitzhugh, Drew Tarter, and Dorothy Wilson, *Sun Herald*

Designer: Brenda Crain, *Crain Creative*

Writers: Kat Bergeron, Ricky Mathews, John McFarland, Dorothy Wilson, Mike Lacy, and other *Sun Herald* staff members

Research: Kat Bergeron, *Sun Herald*

Photographers: James Edward Bates, John C. Fitzhugh, Tim Isbell and David Purdy *Sun Herald*; Drew Tarter, *Sun Herald* photo director; Kim Anderson, Kat Bergeron, Tammy Smith and Pete Tattersall, *Sun Herald* staffers; Reggie Beehner, Kevin Cooper, Sean Loftin, Allison Long, Vernon Matthews, Beth Musgrave, Cara Owsley, Jessica Potts and Kristen Treadwell, former *Sun Herald* staffers; Jared Lazarus, *The Miami Herald*; Pat Sullivan, freelance photographer

Special thanks to the following contributors:
John Wilkerson, freelance photographer, Charles Gray and Eddie Coleman, Hancock County Historical Society; Ray L. Bellande, historian; Biloxi Public Library; Tillman Family; and *Sun Herald* Readers

Technical support: Gretchen O'Boyle, *Sun Herald*

Published by *Sun Herald*, Biloxi, Mississippi

First edition.

ISBN 10: 1-933466-12-X
ISBN 13: 978-1-933466-12-5

Printed in the United States of America
by Walsworth Publishing Co., Marceline, Missouri

To order copies, call 1-800-591-2097
Order on-line at www.sunherald.com

Cover Photograph
THE PALM AFTER THE STORM

The 1840s Father Ryan House on Beach Boulevard, most recently serving as a bed and breakfast, was often described as one of Biloxi's most architecturally important and intriguing houses, the latter because of its legendary palm tree and former resident, the Rev. Abram J. Ryan. Ryan, a Confederate chaplain, gained the title "Poet Laureate of the South" with his poignant poetry. After the war, legend claims Ryan created a religious grotto that included a small palm. As years passed, the grotto disappeared, the house was enlarged and the tree became so huge it seemed to be growing out of the broad front steps. The Father Ryan Palm, as it is called, survived Katrina. The house, however, did not. "The palm tree is a miracle," said Henry Le, the most recent owner who bought the house at auction. "Another miracle is that a statue of Virgin Mary floated to the house and now it sits next to the palm."

BEFORE PHOTOGRAPH: TIM ISBELL
AFTER PHOTOGRAPH: JOHN FITZHUGH

CONTENTS

FOREWORD

From the Publisher
BY RICKY MATHEWS

The efforts to recover, rebuild and renew post-Katrina have brought forth the best in our citizens and leaders. This book is dedicated to the people of South Mississippi and to the mayors, supervisors, city managers, city, state, county employees and volunteers who share the daunting responsibility of facilitating the rebuilding process and enabling us to capture the essence of what has been lost.

Katrina destroyed more than 1,000 historic structures and thousands more were damaged. "This is the worst cultural disaster in American history," said Richard Moe, president of the National Historic Trust, of the damage inflicted upon South Mississippi.

We learned in the wake of Katrina that few incentives were available to the owners of damaged historic structures to help spur them to rebuild. For this reason, the *Sun Herald* has committed $100,000 from the proceeds of its book, *Katrina: 8 Hours That Changed The Mississippi Coast Forever,* to the South Mississippi Preservation Trust Fund for the purpose of providing seed money to help owners of historic properties stabilize and rebuild these important structures.

The history, culture and diversity of this great and beautiful place was captured in the unique architecture of these lost and damaged buildings. Their form and design help to give us our sense of place. As we rebuild, we cannot afford to lose these architectural design elements.

There is no doubt in my mind, in spite of the enormous challenges we face, that by the year 2010, our story of renewal will be the most significant rebuilding story in American history.

God bless the inspiring people of South Mississippi.

PHOTOGRAPH: JAMES EDWARD BATES

INTRODUCTION

Katrina: A Story That Words Could Not Tell
BY KAT BERGERON

"When words become unclear, I shall focus with photographs," the late, great American photographer Ansel Adams observed. It is poignant advice for all who have lived on the Mississippi Gulf Coast, for all who have played here or visited here, for all who realize that Hurricane Katrina destroyed more than buildings, homes and landmarks.

On Aug. 29, 2005, Katrina claimed much that was the region's tangible sense of place – two centuries of charming architecture and vintage oaks as well as modern landmarks that melded the old and the new as South Mississippi marched into the 21st century.

When Richard Moe, head of the Washington, D.C.- based National Trust for Historic Preservation, toured the region in October 2005, he labeled Katrina the worst cultural disaster in U.S. history. In the decades and generations that will follow Katrina, photographs will be the best storytellers. Human memory will disappear, as has the physical evidence taken by Katrina's winds and water. The photographs will continue to communicate powerfully and instantly.

Nothing proves more strongly how important these images are to the human psyche than the *Sun Herald's* Before and After series, created by photographer John C. Fitzhugh. The newspaper feature, which daily highlighted a house, a business, or some other site, included photographs of how the structure looked before-and-after the storm, accompanied by a short story.

Print and online readers immediately clamored for a more permanent Before and After in book form. Justified one requester, "It helps connect the people to their grief, which helps them move forward."

LITTLE RED HOUSE
BILOXI

Katrina was truly an "Equal Opportunity Destroyer," and proof is in the Little Red House, one of the smallest homes on Beach Boulevard. It was four houses west of the Biloxi Lighthouse and was owned by Jane Tipton. Legend claims it was built by an Irishman who didn't manage money well so his possessions became less and less.

"These are sad times for our community. So much loss, so much heartbreak…. Thank you, for a proper tribute," wrote yet another.

Katrina took more than 65,000 housing units, with the numbers doubled for damaged but repairable. Businesses, 70 percent damaged, closed or destroyed immediately after the storm, are slowly coming back, just as building contractors are busy with repairs and new housing.

Katrina claimed public landmarks, beloved kitsch, favorite restaurants, architectural treasures, tourist attractions, museums, schools, libraries, public housing, piers, grave sites, city halls, even hurricane memorials. Small houses, grand houses. Mom-and-pop shops, entire strip malls. The giant oak, the little camellia. The neighborhood church, the big beach front sanctuary.

As the photographs in this book prove, Katrina held nothing sacred.

BY KAT BERGERON

Nine heads popped up like jack-in-the-boxes, followed by giggles of the young and the innocent. The adults laughed — they couldn't help it — but their palms quickly forced the heads down again. Danger lurked in the howling winds.

The nine children, ages 1 to 7, could easily blow off the roof into the raging Katrina waters. The merging of the Gulf and the Jourdan River filled up their Middle Town neighborhood in Waveland like a lake. "We had to protect the babies; that's what we kept thinking," said Jerome Thomas. "We had to make the babies stay down. To them, it was fun. They didn't know what was going on.

"We all prayed to God that there would be no tornadoes."

Ten adults and nine "babies" endured this comic nightmare. The water came to the eaves, and waves splashed higher but the house stayed. At one point, the adults managed to knock a hole in the roof and lift the children down out of the wind. Then, the kids really enjoyed their game

of jack-in-the-box. The adult point of view is scarier.

"From our roof, I could see people hanging onto trees for dear life," said Jerome, at 41, a self-employed laborer. He'd decided to stay alone for Katrina in the house he shared on Herlihy Street with his mother. The family home had always withstood hurricanes, and besides, no water ever came over the

railroad track — and that was three blocks away. Jerome fixed himself a little dinner, watched TV and went to bed about midnight.

"At 2 in the morning, the winds started big and I jumped out of bed and ran to my auntie's," said Jerome. "I wanted to be with my family."

Many had gathered at Aunt Marylee Hall's to weather Katrina.

"By 6, the wind was really rough and everything was flying up and down. Then the water started rushing both ways. When it was about to our chins, we headed to our neighbors'."

Next door, at Gary Hawkins' house, there was a big, flat skiff. They put the children and

elderly in it and when the water rose high enough, they climbed to the safety of the rooftop – and prayed the wind wouldn't knock them off.

Standing up was impossible. In Jerome's words, "The wind was whooping."

They were soaked and shivering. They were up there more than four hours, as best Jerome can remember. Some things remain fuzzy.

When it was safe, they climbed down to survey the destruction of a close-knit, predominately black neighborhood where folks, many of them kin, looked out for each other. Jerome picked his way to his house, but it wasn't

where it was supposed to be. The surge had washed it into his uncle's house next door and partly onto Herlihy Street.

"We have to try to forget everything that happened and go on with our lives," reflected Jerome. "But the next time there's a tropical storm, I'm gone."

"We had to protect the babies; that's what we kept thinking,"

PHOTOGRAPH COURTESY OF CHRISTEL FRITZCHING

PHOTOGRAPH: JOHN FITZHUGH

HARBOR TOWNHOUSES DIAMONDHEAD

Built in 1986, Harbor Townhouses in south Diamondhead was 37 townhouses nestled on Harbor Circle. Peter and Christel Fritzching bought theirs, second from right, in 1999. The south side of Diamondhead included the yacht club, about 250 homes, and these Harbor Townhouses which were destroyed. "It's not so bad," Christel said after the hurricane. "I'm getting to the point it's just stuff and you can replace it. Thankfully, we had insurance and we don't have to live in a little trailer."

ISLANDER MARINA
LAKESHORE

Kirk Ladner's Islander Marina in Lakeshore was the perfect jumping-off spot for fishermen and boaters to enjoy Hancock County's waters. Ladner had traveled around the country, studying marinas with an eye toward what his family would build in Lakeshore, a community west of Waveland. Several years ago, the $2 million Islander Marina opened with both wet and dry dock facilities. Hurricane Katrina didn't leave much of the Islander Marina, but the Ladner family plans to build it back bigger than before.

PHOTOGRAPHS: JOHN FITZHUGH

ST. JOSEPH'S CHAPEL
BAY ST. LOUIS

The land for St. Joseph's Chapel on Dunbar Avenue in Bay St. Louis was formerly part of the Cowand plantation and was sold to the Catholic diocese in the 1890s for $25. Only steps remain of the quaint little chapel that survived 12 hurricanes before Katrina.

The little wooden St. Joseph's Chapel personified small-town churchgoing. Its simple architecture and quiet setting invited worship. It has been the favored marrying, baptizing, burying and christening place of choice for untold Catholics. When Hurricane Camille devastated Bay St.

Louis in 1969, the chapel revived the community's spirit when word spread that as the water retreated out of the sanctuary, it lifted the statues of St. Joseph and the Blessed Mother that flanked the altar and carried them to the front door. There they stood, upright and unchipped.

In 2004, the Biloxi Catholic Diocese cited a shortage of priests and closed the chapel except for special occasions. The St. Joe's loyalists continued to take care of the chapel. Then came Katrina. This time, St. Joe's is not a hurricane survivor.

PHOTOGRAPHS: JOHN WILKERSON

BUCCANEER STATE PARK
WAVELAND

In July 2004, Buccaneer State Park in Waveland was filled with happy water sliders.

In October 2005, Buccaneer's water slide was a ride to nowhere. With a wave pool, pine trails, inviting camper sites and a gorgeous view of the Mississippi Sound, Buccaneer Park was a premier state park for revenue. The gate house, wooden decks, staff residences, office complex and other structures either blew away or washed away. A number of stately pines fell or will become secondary casualties from scarring. Decking around the popular wave pool is gone. The good news is that the pool, built of heavily reinforced concrete, survived.

PHOTOGRAPH: PETE TATTERSALL

PHOTOGRAPH: JOHN FITZHUGH

PHOTOGRAPH: TIM ISBELL

PHOTOGRAPH: JOHN FITZHUGH

In February 2000, like every other day, thousands of cars passed over the bridge between Bay St. Louis and Pass Christian. The bridge over the Bay of St. Louis, like its counterpart over the mouth of Biloxi Back Bay, was demolished by Hurricane Katrina. The bridge photographed here stretches over the Bay of St. Louis from the town of that name to Henderson Point. It was dedicated in 1954 and required considerable repairs after Hurricane Camille. The first automobile bridge across the bay was dedicated in 1929 and was a little south of this one.

In March 2006, work began on a replacement bridge. The ambitious time line calls for two lanes of traffic flowing in May 2007, with completion six months later.

PHOTOGRAPHS: JOHN FITZHUGH

WAVELAND CITY HALL

Waveland City Hall was nestled among the trees on Coleman Avenue. In October 2005, the building was replaced by a Quonset hut and little was left of a nearby tree. City Hall, built in 1888 and the only building on the south half of Coleman Avenue to survive Hurricane Camille in 1969, recently underwent a $400,000 renovation. "We certainly do plan to build back City Hall," said Waveland Mayor Tommy Longo. "Some want to build back as close to history as we can, and some want to blend the old and the new. It's something we'll work out."

PHOTOGRAPHS: JOHN FITZHUGH

Waveland is so proud of its Garfield Ladner Memorial Pier that it often uses the image in national promotions for the town of 7,000-plus known for its beachfront and laid-back lifestyle.

Garfield Pier was touted by the city as the only lighted pier with 24-hour security that allowed people to fish, read, walk and talk any time of the day. It was named after a longtime mayor who was at the city's helm when Hurricane Camille struck in 1969. "We'd just finished the comfort station and eight pagoda-shaped picnic areas," said Mayor Tommy Longo. "Positively, we are going to rebuild Garfield Pier. It is an identity for this community."

ST. CLARE CATHOLIC CHURCH WAVELAND

St. Clare Catholic Church, 236 South Beach Blvd., Waveland, was a parish of 800 when this photograph was taken in 2003. Since Hurricane Katrina, St. Clare Catholic Church has had services in a Quonset hut set up on the church foundation. The minister is living in a travel trailer. The rectory and church will be rebuilt on the same foundations.

PHOTOGRAPH: REGGIE BEEHNER

PHOTOGRAPH: JOHN FITZHUGH

PHOTOGRAPHS: JOHN FITZHUGH

OLD MCDONALD HOUSE
BAY ST. LOUIS

The Queen Ann house high on a bluff at 502 North Beach Blvd. was a Bay St. Louis architectural gem. The 14-foot ceilings, intricate Victorian Gothic woodwork, and wrap-around porch were constructed in 1889 by Charles Sanger, whose stamp was on the original St. Stanislaus College, St. Joseph's Academy, and courthouse. In 2000, Kevin and Sherrye Webster bought the "Old McDonald House," named for the family that had owned it since 1904. When the Websters restored the outside and downstairs, they opened it for a fund-raising tour, and again when the upstairs was finished. "I feel that we are the keepers of these old houses, and my greatest wish was that when I'm long gone that the house would still be there," Sherrye Webster said. "The charm of Bay St. Louis was its houses." Katrina wrecked the house. "When I first saw it I was waiting for Tina Turner to come out in a Mad Max movie," Webster said. "My heart is broken, not for our stuff, that was material, but for the town of Bay St. Louis and for the people."

PHOTOGRAPHS: JOHN WILKERSON

BAY TOWN INN
BAY ST. LOUIS

In 1999, the DeMontluzin house that became Bay Town Inn Bed & Breakfast in Bay St. Louis turned 100 years old. Fulfilling a dream of owning a business that would use her knack of making people feel welcome and her love of gardening and cooking, Nikki Nicholson moved from New Orleans and bought Bay Town Inn Bed & Breakfast in 2003. The art and antique-filled B&B at 208 North Beach Blvd., was swept away. On the property stand two oaks, including the one that saved Nicholson, a dog, and two others who made it to the tree when the 1899 house disintegrated. Built by the DeMontluzin family, the 4,600-square-foot house had eight guest rooms and a cottage.

JIMMY RUTHERFORD PIER
BAY ST. LOUIS

With its attractive mini-pavilions for socializing and inviting fishing opportunities, Jimmy Rutherford Pier at Ulman Avenue was a focal point of the Bay St. Louis waterfront. The concrete pier opened in 1998, thanks to more than $400,000 in Tideland Funds grant money, and with another expansion in 2002, it reached at least 1,400 feet into the Bay of St. Louis. Katrina's destruction is only temporary. "Ulman Avenue pier will be rebuilt," said Mayor Eddie Favre."
The pier wasn't just for fishing. People used it for almost everything. They'd exercise on it, sit and relax on it, get married on it. It's important to incorporate the rebuilt pier with some of the Governor's Commission (on Rebuilding, Recovery and Renewal) ideas."

PHOTOGRAPHS: JOHN FITZHUGH

DIAMONDHEAD YACHT CLUB

Opened in 1975, the distinctive Tiki-hut shape of the Diamondhead Yacht Club is in keeping with Diamondhead's Hawaiian theme. A stylized representation of the shape is seen on Diamondhead residents' car stickers, a shape inspired by the extinct volcano on the island of Oahu. The decor, the brainchild of developer Purcell Co., extended to the country club and even to some homes in the gated community. Katrina's storm surge left little more than the yacht club's roof. The Ship's Store, a separate building alongside, and many piers and slips of the marina simply disappeared. The Diamondhead Property Owners' Association is considering rebuilding, leasing to a restaurateur, or possibly restoring it to its former glory.

BIENVILLE STATUE
BAY ST. LOUIS

A statue of French explorer Bienville, who led an expedition to find the mouth of the Mississippi River and discovered the Bay of St. Louis along the way, was unveiled in 1999 on the 300th anniversary. The sculpture by Coast artist Mary Ott Davidson survived Hurricane Katrina, though much else that was Tercentenary Park did not. The historic Hancock Bank building beside it is one of the few Front Beach survivors. As any local schoolchild could tell you, a Frenchman named Iberville is responsible for settlement of the Mississippi Coast in 1699. What many may not know is that this Pierre Le Moyne, sieur d'Iberville, had a brother named Jean Baptiste le Moyne, sieur de Bienville. Bienville was an adventurer, explorer, soldier and bit of a politician like his better-known older brother. He was the one in 1699 who first stepped on the shore of Bay St. Louis and named the area for his king's patron saint.

PHOTOGRAPH: CARA OWSLEY

PHOTOGRAPH: JOHN FITZHUGH

COLEMAN AVENUE AT BEACH BOULEVARD WAVELAND

Wavelanders like to find excuses to line their main thoroughfares, among them the corner of Coleman Avenue and Beach Boulevard. Here before Katrina, at Easter time 2005, they gather for Paws on Parade, a fund-raiser for the Hancock County Animal Shelter. Wavelanders love their Irish and Mardi Gras parades and such things as Paws on Parade. They also prefer to prop their feet on porch rails or wet a hook to making noteworthy waves. Katrina changed that, at least for now, because Waveland is one of the ground-zero cities. When the hurricane hit, the population was listed at 6,674, although city fathers say growth mushroomed in the five years since the 2000 census. "What was nice about Waveland is that it was a small town but it was cosmopolitan," said Georgia Goodell.

COURT STREET STATION
BAY ST. LOUIS

The corner of Court Street and South Beach began as a large 19th century hotel, which burned in 1927. Little did Andre Arceneaux realize that when he opened his gas service station here in the 1930s that the location would claim a tiny spot of movie history. When Natalie Wood filmed part of *This Property is Condemned* in the Bay, the actress parked her car under the shade of a tree there. Since the Arceneaux family closed their full-service station, Court Street Station has undergone numerous renovations and has served many duties, including as an antique shop, flea market, lounge and assorted restaurants.

PHOTOGRAPHS: JOHN WILKERSON

PHOTOGRAPH: JAMES EDWARD BATES

MYERS HOME
WAVELAND

Talk about a double whammy. In June 2001, Bill Myers was brushing his teeth when he heard an explosion, walked into his living room at 120 Lafitte Drive, and found a Cessna 172RG fuselage in the middle of it and the mangled nose of the airplane sticking out from the front of the brick house. The pilot, on a fish-spotting expedition, did not survive, and Myers, a lay Episcopal minister, gave him last rites. "I kinda think that God was preparing us for a total loss," observes Linda Myers.

They had repaired everything when Katrina took their home of 20 years. The Myers are in limbo as to whether they will build back in the friendly neighborhood known for block parties.

PHOTOGRAPH: JOHN FITZHUGH

KENNEY HOME
LAKESHORE

Bayou Caddy Marina in Lakeshore was built with state tideland's lease monies in the late 1990s, and that, in a nice twist of circumstance, is how Robert "Capt. Bob" Kenney found his dream house at 5011 Lambert Lane. He brought his 72-foot Aimee Lynn there for fuel and spotted the house for sale, perfect because he could dock his shrimp trawler on his own pier. In Katrina, the Kenneys lost that house, two others, two vehicles, three boats, but not the Aimee Lynn. They're living in a FEMA trailer in Slidell, near the seafood business they started and that is now run by family. "We miss being in Lakeshore and we miss shrimping," said Linda. "We could never build back for what insurance pays us. We want to live back there and I think we will. It was the perfect place, the last house on the beach road in Mississippi."

PHOTOGRAPH: JAMES EDWARD BATES

PHOTOGRAPH: JOHN FITZHUGH

PHOTOGRAPHS: JOHN WILKERSON

WARD HOME
BAY ST. LOUIS

Early settlers put a cemetery on this land, but after graves kept getting washed away in storms, the remaining ones were moved to Cedar Rest, where the oldest headstones date to the 1820s. Some historians also think this to be the site of Camp Good, a Civil War encampment.

Eventually, a Spanish-style stucco house was built here but destroyed in Camille in 1969. The front porch of that house stood until the late 1990s, when Ron Ward, a retired river pilot, built the large brick colonial at 812 South Beach Blvd.

MAGNOLIA MARKET
BAY ST. LOUIS

The day before Katrina, photographer John Wilkerson captured the image of Magnolia Market, a long-time boutique and antique mall at the corner of Main Street and North Beach. It was prepared for the storm with state-of-the-art metal storm shutters. After the storm, he returned to the same corner and found the exposed manhole cover, about 5 feet tall, and missing beach road.

PHOTOGRAPHS: JOHN WILKERSON

OLD TOWN
BAY ST. LOUIS

Like a magnet, Old Town draws locals and tourists to Hancock County to play, eat, shop or just soak up the laid-back waterfront atmosphere that is Old Town's trademark. With an eclectic mix of architecture, eateries, shops and art galleries, people returned for more, gladly parking and walking the distance down North and South Beach Boulevard and up Main Street. Old Town is and intends to remain a while-away-the-hours kind of place. This aerial, taken in 1992, captures Old Town at its charming best. Waterside buildings were anchored at the right by Dock of the Bay and The Good Life on the left. Facing buildings from left of the railroad tracks include Court Street Station, Fire Dog Saloon, Chessy's antiques, Hancock Bank, Magnolia Mall, Trapani's Eatery, the old A&G Theater and the Old Coffee Pot.

PHOTOGRAPH: JOHN FITZHUGH

PHOTOGRAPHS: JOHN WILKERSON

BEACHWOOD HALL
BAY ST. LOUIS

Beachwood Hall at 806 South Beach Blvd., circa 1840, was built by Dominic Gregnon, who liked the design so well that he built three just alike, in a row. The 1947 hurricane got one, Camille another, and Beachwood Hall was claimed by Katrina. Former owner and noted Hancock County historian Charles Gray called the house a "preservation rather than restoration" because it was never allowed to run down. Beachwood Hall was the center of many home tours and lavish entertainment, and several years ago Gray sold it to, oddly enough, a man named Charles Gary.

GULFSIDE ASSEMBLY
WAVELAND

When blacks were refused the right to swim on most Mississippi beaches, Gulfside Assembly became a mecca. On its waterfront in Waveland, children and adults of color could safely swim, fish and crab. Gulfside, created by black Methodists in 1924, was one of the few places in the segregated South where blacks could do this.

Gulfside became a 60-acre retreat where visitors — black and white — participated in programs of education, spiritual nurturing and family support. Then came Katrina. All the buildings were leveled. "Gulfside is a centerpiece for the traditionally black church and there is a lot of sentimental attachment to the grounds," said the Rev. Jerry Beam, district superintendent of Seashore United Methodist District. "I know the Southeast Jurisdiction is meeting about Gulfside's future role."

PHOTOGRAPH: CARA OWSLEY

PHOTOGRAPH: JOHN FITZHUGH

PHOTOGRAPHS: JOHN WILKERSON

ELMWOOD MANOR
BAY ST. LOUIS

Construction on Elmwood Manor, 900 North Beach Blvd. began about 1804, and was part of Jesse Cowand's 553-acre plantation that specialized in Sea Island cotton. The two-story house with West Indies architecture was built out of ship ballast bricks. It had a series of owners determined to restore one of the Bay's most historically significant houses, but always the job was daunting because the brick was soft, absorbed moisture, and caused mildew inside. The latest owners, Jim and Catherine MacPhaille, who bought it several months before Katrina, had gotten expert advice on how to solve that problem.

DA BEACH HOUSE
BAY ST. LOUIS

This eclectic combined eatery and beach rental helped the Bay live up to its laid-back reputation. Bicycles for riding on the beach and assorted boats for cruising the water, Da Beach House had it all. Owners Colleen and Todd Read described 604 South Beach Blvd. as "the complete beach experience." People hung out, got fresh fruit smoothies, ate bagels and rented a kayak. A person could even buy local art, join a poetry reading, or a drumming circle. "We are going to try to bring back to life a few of our events," Colleen said, "but our location is completely gone. It will take time to figure things out."

PHOTOGRAPHS: JOHN WILKERSON

HERON HOME
WAVELAND

Paul and Stella La Violette built Heron Home at 665 North Beach Blvd., in 1976, and bestowed that name because herons danced, mated and fought, as if putting on a show for them. "We felt this was the Great Blue Herons home, not just the house but the property and the beach," said La Violette, a marine scientist who let his writing and poetry muse blossom after retiring. Each summer, a friend would come and together they would build more, doubling the original 3,000 square feet: "The house fit exactly the way Stella and I wanted, so that in every room you could see the beach and there was a middle glass atrium." The La Violettes say they could never rebuild such a large home, and may not be able to afford to rebuild at all because of property taxes. "The Coast is being pressured by condo developments that are pushing up property values of houses and I'm a retiree on a limited income," La Violette said. In addition to that, as a marine scientist he wants "to see what this next season of storms is like."

WARD HOME
BAY ST. LOUIS

The owner of this post-Camille house, Dr. Swan Ward, at one time a physician for Stennis Space Center, styled it after a New Orleans double shotgun. The 982 Beach Blvd., house was at the corner of the beach and Bay Oaks Drive, so named because of its proliferation of Live Oaks. Bay St. Louis had 576 houses on the National Register of Historic Places. Katrina totaled 228, and preservation of 40 others is uncertain.

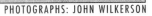
PHOTOGRAPHS: JOHN WILKERSON

DEJA VIEW
WAVELAND

Deja View is a Mediterranean-style house built by Roland Hymel Jr. of New Orleans at 711 North Beach Blvd. His parents' summer house, Fair Oaks, was on the same land but was destroyed by Camille. He rebuilt on the beach front about 1990 using huge round cement columns embedded in the ground and a stone wall, all with future storms in mind.

JEFFERY HOME
WAVELAND

Some who built after Hurricane Camille designed homes with storms in mind. This house of Betty Jeffery at 705 North Beach Blvd. was constructed on the property of her parents whose house was destroyed by Camille in 1969. It used steel pilings and some of the refurbished original columns from her parents' house. The ground and first floors were swept through by Katrina but parts of the third floor remained. The steel beams withstood.

PHOTOGRAPHS: JOHN WILKERSON

LEE-WATERMAN HOUSE
BAY ST. LOUIS

The Lee-Waterman House at 143 St. Charles, circa 1890, is owned by John S. Waterman IV, featuring an L-shaped shotgun, one of the typical 1890s Creole cottages with front and side gallery. It is being restored.

PHOTOGRAPHS: HANCOCK COUNTY HISTORICAL SOCIETY

GIARDINO HOME
BAY ST. LOUIS

Dr. Marco Giardino, a specialist in NASA space imaging, owned the 1915 gable-on-hip-roofed cottage with undercut gallery that had to be bulldozed. It was at 147 St. Charles St.

PHOTOGRAPHS: HANCOCK COUNTY HISTORICAL SOCIETY

CARVER HOME
BAY. ST. LOUIS

Ashton Carver owned this circa 1900 L-plan shotgun cottage with front and side galleries destroyed by Katrina. It was at 202 St. Charles St.

THRIFFILEY HOME
BAY ST. LOUIS

Katrina took the home that orthopedic surgeon Jim Thriffiley IV and wife Angie lived in at 1908 North Beach Blvd. although it wasn't theirs. They'd sold it but awaited completion of their dream house three doors down. The houses, their possessions and his office medical equipment are gone. For now, they're not rebuilding.

HECKER HOME
BAY ST. LOUIS

Before Katrina, no one thought a great deal about this little house at 220 North Beach Blvd. Like 576 other houses in the Bay, it was on the National Register and was dated 1893 as a residence. The hurricane revealed its real history, stripping away the more "modern" facade. Now the Hancock County Historical Society considers it one of the most interesting little houses, at 10 feet by 30 feet, on the Registry. Fallen walls have revealed hand-hewn timbers and lathing, and horse-hair plaster and parts of a house thought to date to the 1780s, making it one of South Mississippi's oldest structures. Although it cannot be rebuilt, the Hecker family that owns it has donated the pieces to be used in the construction of a museum. The National Trust for Historic Preservation and others are undertaking its disassembly.

LAPINE HOME
BAY ST. LOUIS

The 1935 one-story, front-gable house at 215 Ballentine St. was owned by Raymond Lapine and typical of that era's half-across-the-front porches. It could not be repaired.

**WILLIAMSON HOME
BAY ST. LOUIS**

The circa 1925 gabled cottage clad with stucco was owned by E.L. Williamson and could not be saved. It was at 223 Ballentine St.

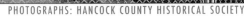
PHOTOGRAPHS: HANCOCK COUNTY HISTORICAL SOCIETY

**PHILLIPS HOME
BAY ST. LOUIS**

Owned by Dorothy Phillips, this circa 1850 house at 222 North Beach Blvd. is being restored with help from the World Monuments Fund and Preservation Trades Network through the Mississippi Heritage Trust.

PHOTOGRAPHS: HANCOCK COUNTY HISTORICAL SOCIETY

MCCANDLES HOME
BAY ST. LOUIS

Noted artist Patti Banister built this 1978 cottage on the former site of Christ Episcopal Church, which was destroyed in Camille. Owner William McCandles plans to restore the house at 226 North Beach Blvd.

CAKE WALK
BAY ST. LOUIS

Cake Walk, at 209 Ballentine St., is a 1915, one-story shotgun cottage owned by Lee McDonough. The home was surrounded by a large retaining wall with enclosed garden.

SEALS HOME
BAY ST. LOUIS

The family home of banker Leo Seals, a circa 1900 colonial revival, will be restored, although the road in front of it is missing. At one time, the house at 408 North Beach Blvd. belonged to Charles Marshal, president of L& N Railroad.

PHOTOGRAPHS: HANCOCK COUNTY HISTORICAL SOCIETY

WHITFIELD HOUSE
BAY ST. LOUIS

Known as Whitfield House, the family of the late Miss Ada Whitfield say they hope to build another house upon the surviving back rooms of the circa 1910 cottage at 610 North Beach Blvd.

PHOTOGRAPHS: HANCOCK COUNTY HISTORICAL SOCIETY

MONET-BREATH HOUSE
BAY ST. LOUIS

616 North Beach Blvd., in the Breath family for four generations, dates to 1814. Originally a Creole cottage, a north wing was added in 1890 and a turret in 1909, so it was listed as a Queen Anne style. A brick French fort under the house had no historical records to explain its existence.

OLD SPANISH CUSTOMS HOUSE
BAY ST. LOUIS

708 South Beach Blvd. was never a customs house, but it housed the inspector who used a boat for duty on the Chandeleur Islands. Built in 1787 of brick baked on the site, it was thought to be the second or third oldest house on the Coast. All that is left of owner Julie Martin's extensive restoration is a pile of bricks, which she is donating to a new Bay museum.

CARROLL PLANTATION HOUSE
BAY ST. LOUIS

224 North Beach Blvd. was part of a working cotton plantation before the Civil War. The circa 1840 house sits on a 31-foot bluff, one of the Coast's highest, and that may be why the Gex family will be able to restore it.

SWOOP MANOR
BAY ST. LOUIS

414 South Beach Blvd., a 1853 Greek Revival, was built by a Spaniard who returned home when his sons died of malaria. Since 1880, it's been in the hands of Julian M. Swoop and descendants, one of the oldest families of the "New Orleans Colony" with summer homes in the Bay.

PHOTOGRAPHS: HANCOCK COUNTY HISTORICAL SOCIETY

PHOTOGRAPHS: HANCOCK COUNTY HISTORICAL SOCIETY

FEOLA HANGAR AND HOME
DIAMONDHEAD

Mario Feola says he applied his knowledge of aeronautical engineering when building his Diamondhead home in 1991 at 23101 Coelho Way. The bottom floor is basically a guest room and a hangar – he and wife Charlotte are pilots – and the top living floor offers a view of the runway. He says it was designed to withstand 150 mph winds with the bottom walls designed to blow out, but they weren't anticipating the water. Feola is vice president of the Diamondhead Property Owner's Association, chartered as a corporation and run by a board for the 3,600 residences. About 250 were made uninhabitable on the south side, Feola said, and about 460 on the north side.

C.C. MCDONALD HOUSE
BAY ST. LOUIS

Known as the C.C. McDonald House, circa 1890, this partial Colonial Revival at 406 North Beach Blvd. was on the market before Katrina and the new owner Ramey Hines has restoration underway.

A&G THEATER
BAY ST. LOUIS

In 1927, the A&G Theater opened at 120 North Beach Blvd., the same year a fire burned everything in the block but A&G, although it left a permanent crack in the wall. Named after two women, Ames and Gaspard, its now in the Maggie Dantagnan Hayden estate, and heirs have made no decisions on its future.

PHOTOGRAPHS: JOHN WILKERSON

MAIN STREET UNITED METHODIST CHURCH
BAY ST. LOUIS

Main Street Methodist survived with a cracked wall and ruined interiors, but the Rev. Rick Brooks knows how lucky he is with more than 80 Coast churches destroyed or badly damaged. After the storm, Brooks told this story: "One of my neighbors ...saw somebody on a bulldozer a few days after the storm. I'm not sure if the young man was with the National Guard or not. This fella has lived and breathed Bay St. Louis most of his life. The church, the sanctuary, has been here 105 years. Katrina blew the steeple onto Second Street. And the guy on the bulldozer was getting pretty ambitious with his project. He was about to discard it. My neighbor came out and objected. Strongly. Apparently, they weren't listening. So he came out with his pistol." The steeple was saved.

PHOTOGRAPHS: JOHN WILKERSON

"The only thing that saved me is that Jesus loves me."

BY KAT BERGERON

A battered, exhausted, bleeding John Porter used his belt to tie himself to a tree as appliances, debris and the occasional person washed by, caught up in the Katrina surge.

HARRISON COUNTY

His flimsy savior tree wasn't a giant Biloxi trademark oak but it provided a small branch platform to stand on to keep his head above water between crashing, 20-plus-foot waves.

He'd suffered through a lot to get there but relief at finding safe footing turned to horror when John realized worse danger lay ahead. Debris and a receding surge would wash him off his branch into the sea.

Each time a breakaway casino barge banged into the 1927 tower of the old Tivoli Hotel, bricks flew his way and he ducked. When the six-story hotel didn't crumble under the abuse, he realized the Tivoli was his chance.

Letting loose of the tree, John headed there. When his feet touched hardness, he thought it was the parking lot, climbed into the nearest window and fell about 15 feet. It wasn't the first floor. That had washed out. It also wasn't the parking lot. It was a lower floor outcropping. The water was still that high. "The only thing that saved me is that Jesus loves me," said the 50-year-old not normally given to religious expression.

Exhausted beyond imagination, John found a muddy blanket, wrapped up in it and slept. Hours later, three others who'd survived by retreating to the Old Tivoli found John wrapped in the blanket and thought him dead.

Tony Olier, who'd carried possessions into the old hotel before the storm, shared with John some clothes, a tomato, a candy bar, and cigarettes. The lucky Tivoli four chatted, even laughed at defeating Katrina.

Then came the dawning. The others? What had happened to the others staying at the Little Tivoli, the residential motel next-door? At least 15 had spent the night there, some playing cards, some sharing drinks, all believing that because both Tivolis had survived Camille they'd be ok.

The Little Tivoli, a 1950s-era, two-story brick-concrete structure, offered a laid-back, very affordable beach lifestyle. Its residents worked in restaurants, casinos and day labor jobs. All didn't live at the Tivoli but had gathered there for the storm, including John, who worked at an oyster house and lived nearby.

At least nine of the 15 died. The survivors included the four in the Old Tivoli and at least two others pulled by John to safety on a refrigerator and plywood.

The tragedy of the Tivoli will remain a storm story tweaked and revived in coming years as more like John share their memories. "I'm not a publicity seeker. I don't want to sensationalize what happened," said John, a Vietnam-era ex-Marine who, before Katrina thought he'd seen it all.

Six months after the storm, with emotion-filled eyes, John stood near the debris-strewn grounds of the Little Tivoli. The slab and huge chunks of walls and ceilings lay there, undisturbed. "Look at that solid concrete," John pointed. "Nobody could have thought it would be like this. We were so cavalier. Don't be a fool like me and the rest. When they say evacuate, do it."

PHOTOGRAPH: TIM ISBELL

PHOTOGRAPH: ALLISON LONG

PHOTOGRAPH: JOHN FITZHUGH

BILOXI LIGHTHOUSE

The Biloxi Lighthouse, a cast-iron tower on the National Register of Historic Places right in the middle of U.S. 90, is considered one of Biloxi's most valuable historic properties. When built in 1848, the light shone 13 miles to sea. It had reopened for public tours in 2005 after being closed for two years. Despite early rumors to the contrary, the lighthouse, which had survived 17 previous hurricanes, also had survived Katrina. Water carried away some sand from the foundation and the surge likely gave the tower a push to the northeast. But, it is stable, and the bricks damaged by the storm can be replaced.

PHOTOGRAPHS: JOHN FITZHUGH

PHOTOGRAPH: DAVID PURDY

PHOTOGRAPH: JOHN FITZHUGH

LONG BEACH BEACH FRONT

The stretch of beach at the Pass Christian-Long Beach line in Harrison county was an inviting and quiet place to relax. But Hurricane Katrina was no kinder to the 27-mile man-made sand beach than it was to the houses, churches and businesses alongside it.

BILOXI BEACH FRONT

From Spring Break to Labor Day, Biloxi beach caters to locals and visitors and other sun worshipers happy enough for a white beach that does not have crashing waves because it borders the Mississippi Sound, not the Gulf. These images include the Lighthouse Pier.

SCENIC DRIVE
PASS CHRISTIAN

In June 2000, Mrs. Mississippi United States 2000, Gilda Seymour of Ocean Springs, ran along Scenic Drive in Pass Christian during a fund-raiser. The elevated street parallels U.S. 90 and the ancient oaks that line it were green glitter on the beautiful homes, gardens and waterfront views that made Scenic Drive a polished Mississippi Coast emerald. Some of the 85 houses on this 2-mile stretch were built before the Civil War; others date from the turn of the 20th century. All, no matter the size, became the stuff of home and architectural magazines. Scenic Drive is one of three sites in the United States designated as a national historic street. Many oak trees along Scenic Drive still stand after Hurricane Katrina, though only time will tell how many will survive the salt and wind.

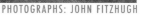

PHOTOGRAPHS: JOHN FITZHUGH

PHOTOGRAPH: JAMES EDWARD BATES

PHOTOGRAPH: JOHN FITZHUGH

TREASURE BAY CASINO BILOXI

Even non-gamblers noticed Treasure Bay Casino when it opened in 1994. It was impossible to miss the "pirate ship," a transformed casino barge, looming so close to shore on the Biloxi Strip. The ship appeared repeatedly on national TV before Hurricane Katrina as a backdrop to weather reports. The storm moved the casino off its mooring and farther west, gutting the first floor. The second floor was largely intact and 400 slot machines and other equipment were salvaged. Much of the first floor was strewn in the Mississippi Sound and is already recovered. One of the "pirates" made of waterproof material washed ashore in front of the home of a restaurant owner and sits on the bar of the renamed Shady's New World Cuisine restaurant.

J.L. SCOTT AQUARIUM
BILOXI

J.L. Scott Aquarium & Marine Education Center opened in 1984 on Biloxi's Point Cadet, attracting locals and tourists who wanted to observe Mississippi's coastal life. The center's education outreach touched thousands. It featured big and small aquariums, a touch tank, gift shop and large shell collection. Katrina severely damaged the building, which has been scheduled for demolition since mid-September. Endangered-species artifacts, some research and equipment were salvaged from the second floor after the storm. Scott is included in the Gulf Coast Research Laboratory's budget, but the University of Southern Mississippi administers GCRL. That brings the Institution of Higher Learning, which oversees state universities, into the picture. Scott director Sharon Walker said the IHL board may not rebuild at Point Cadet. Before Katrina, the center planned a new 79,400-square-foot aquarium facility, designed after J.L. Scott's overseers had agreed the center's prime waterfront site would be used for education. Now, IHL with USM and GCRL have one year to decide what to do.

PHOTOGRAPH: DREW TARTER

PHOTOGRAPH: DAVID PURDY

PHOTOGRAPHS: JOHN FITZHUGH

BILOXI SMALL CRAFT HARBOR

Beginning with Capt. Louis Gorenflo a half-century ago, the Sailfish, a 42-foot wooden double-decker, has changed owners several times but continues to be a hallmark of Coast tourism.

Most recently, Capt. Virginia Eleuterius and her husband Corrie bought the Sailfish tour business in 1994. As a youngster, Corrie had watched the Sailfish being constructed across the street from his grandmother's house. Now it's his. "We both captain the boat," said his wife, "but Corrie is the show. He loves entertaining with stories about this area and what comes up in the net." The SailFish has returned to its berth at The Biloxi Small Craft Harbor. The Biloxi Shrimp Trip was reinstated and the harbor will be rebuilt.

MCCAUGHAN HOUSE
LONG BEACH

The Harper McCaughan House at 126 East 4th St. in Long Beach was built in 1908. Owner Alyce Scoggins said a tornado in Hurricane Katrina claimed the porch, winds battered it elsewhere and the surge brought in 2 feet of water. Seven feet of debris landed in the yard, including a boat.

PHOTOGRAPHS COURTESY OF WESLEY SCOGGINS

LONG BEACH LOOKOUT RESTAURANT

The Long Beach Lookout, formerly Fish 'N Bones, opened in 2002. It stood atop stilts in the Long Beach Small Craft Harbor and featured fresh grilled seafood and what owner Rob Stinson described as "the most panoramic view of the ocean and the beach." From its opening to the day Katrina landed, the number of customers quadrupled. Katrina wiped the building away. But, fearing he would lose his staff, Stinson reopened in Gulfport less than five weeks after the storm and hopes to re-open at the harbor.

PHOTOGRAPH: TIM ISBELL

PHOTOGRAPH: JOHN FITZHUGH

PHOTOGRAPH: JAMES EDWARD BATES

PHOTOGRAPH: JOHN FITZHUGH

GREAT SOUTHERN GOLF CLUB
GULFPORT

Capt. Joseph T. Jones wanted a fitting golf clubhouse to go with his new Great Southern Hotel, and in 1908 it and a state-of-the-art golf course appeared several miles away, in what was then unincorporated land between Biloxi and Gulfport. The distinctive roofed clubhouse, even visited by President Woodrow Wilson on a stay here, was preserved and maintained as different companies took over ownership. A group of members eventually bought the Great Southern Golf Club, both the historic building and the beachfront course.

MISSISSIPPI CITY COURTHOUSE GULFPORT

The Mississippi City Courthouse sat in the first capital of Harrison County but now is incorporated into Gulfport. The courthouse complex started in 1841 with the birth of the county. It was built in 1893 and housed records, a grand jury room and clerks' offices. "The city saved the bricks that were salvageable," said Mayor Brent Warr. "The plan is to rebuild and restore the building to as close to its original condition as possible." The remaining part is a modern addition built to mold with the old.

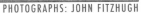

PHOTOGRAPHS: JOHN FITZHUGH

PHOTOGRAPH: TIM ISBELL

BEAUVOIR
BILOXI

Beauvoir was the last home of Confederate President Jefferson Davis. It was built in 1852-54 for James Brown, a Madison County cotton planter. Lavish frescoed interior walls and ceilings, rounded corners, Greek revival mantels and other details make Beauvoir an architectural treasure. The new presidential library was gutted and the Confederate Veterans Hospital swept away, as were the two front pavilions, but the big house is stable though badly damaged. The front and back galleries, or porches, are gone or collapsed, as is a parlor wall and ceiling. Preliminary figures are that restoration of the house and presidential library will cost $25 million, and the Mississippi Sons of Confederate Veterans, which owns the property, will do fund-raising. Furnishings are undergoing conservation and the hunt for museum offices is still under way on Beauvoir property.

PHOTOGRAPH: DREW TARTER

SS CAMILLE GIFT SHOP GULFPORT

There weren't many things on West Beach Boulevard in Gulfport that didn't get swept away by Hurricane Katrina. Ironically, one of the few landmarks surviving is the SS Hurricane Camille. The 72-foot tugboat East Point, washed ashore by the 1969 storm that changed its name, remains right where it was, although worse for wear. Lucille Moody, who owned it and the Hurricane Camille Gift Shop behind it, said she found three new holes in the hull and a dent in the bow. She said she doesn't plan to rebuild the gift store now.

PHOTOGRAPH: TIM ISBELL

PHOTOGRAPH: JOHN FITZHUGH

GRAND CASINO
BILOXI

Grand Casino Biloxi has grown in spurts since its opening in January 1994, a growth reflected in one of the largest gambling barges among the Coast's 13 casinos in business at the time of Katrina. The hurricane swept the Grand, now part of Harrah's Entertainment, across U.S. 90. The Grand plans to reopen on Casino Row in mid-summer, this time with the gambling taking place in a land hotel because the state, post-Katrina, approved land-based gambling.

PHOTOGRAPHS: DAVID PURDY

CASINO PAWN
BILOXI

Point Cadet Pawn was no ordinary pawn shop. The building, which sat atop its own mini-hill across the street from the east end of Biloxi's Casino Row, was filled with stuff — all kinds of interesting Mississippi Coast memorabilia that made it a mini-museum as well as a place to find bargains or make emergency sales when money needs arose.

"I promise you, it was a jewel of the South," said Kenneth Bond, who with Dr. John W. Godsey, opened the shop in 1999. Before that, Godsey had run the building as an antique shop. The Casino Magic barge came to final rest near the pawn shop.

PHOTOGRAPHS: JOHN FITZHUGH

PHOTOGRAPH: KRISTEN TREADWELL

PHOTOGRAPH: JOHN FITZHUGH

THE CRAWFORD HOUSE
BILOXI

The Crawford House in October 2001 was an integral part of the Tullis-Toledano complex in Biloxi. The core of the Crawford House was thought to date to the 1850s when its better-known beachfront neighbor, Tullis-Toledano Manor, was built. It was thought to be a carriage house made of red brick that matched the manor. Hurricane Katrina left only a pile of bricks where the Crawford House stood.

TULLIS-TOLEDANO MANOR BILOXI

Tullis-Toledano Manor, a 19th-century antebellum home in Biloxi made of red-clay bricks from this region, was not as grand as some architecture from the 1850s, but its history reflects Biloxi culture. Hurricane Camille badly damaged the manor in 1969. During restoration, the city returned it and the slave quarters near it to their original appearance, using them as a museum and popular site for weddings and local gatherings. Hurricane Katrina, showing no respect to Tullis-Toledano, forced the Grand Casino Biloxi barge on top of the house site.

PHOTOGRAPHS: JOHN FITZHUGH

OHR-O'KEEFE MUSEUM OF ART AND PLEASANT REED HOUSE BILOXI

The 1887 Pleasant Reed House was the only known remaining Mississippi Coast home of a former slave and it was the cornerstone of the Ohr-O'Keefe Museum of Art's emphasis on African-American culture.

The Reed family story echoes the black experience. At 35, Reed became a land owner and later felt so strongly about his rights that he'd work an extra day to pay his poll tax and vote. Reed House was destroyed, and through the wind-stripped trees, the Frank Gehry-designed Center for Ceramics is more visible now. The center will be the first part of the new Ohr-O'Keefe Museum of Art, scheduled to open in 2007.

BILOXI VISITOR CENTER

The Visitor Center on the Town Green in downtown Biloxi was comprised of the architecturally intricate Brielmaier House in front and the minimalist Foretich House in back. The Brielmaier House was built about 1895 with much of the woodwork by Paul W. Brielmaier. He turned it into a woodworking masterpiece. Both houses were moved to the Town Green and restored in the late 1980s. At least 50,000 locals and visitors came to the center every year to ask questions about the city, find out about lodging, hotels and attractions or attend one of the festivals or holiday events. After Hurricane Katrina, nothing was left of the houses but substructure.

PHOTOGRAPH: DAVID PURDY

PHOTOGRAPH: JOHN FITZHUGH

69

ANNIE'S RESTAURANT HENDERSON POINT

Annie's restaurant on Henderson Point near Pass Christian, with its famous fried chicken and angel-hair pasta with marinara sauce, opened in 1928. It was rebuilt five times, after three hurricanes and two fires. However, Hurricane Katrina destroyed the restaurant. "This wasn't a restaurant. This was a family. It was a wonderful way of life," said "Miss Annie" Lutz, whose parents opened the restaurant, which may or may not return to the site.

BILOXI BEACH AMUSEMENT PARK

Rex was a popular 15-foot dinosaur at Biloxi Beach Amusement Park and an icon of Hurricane Camille survival. But Hurricane Katrina broke Rex into green pieces and destroyed the rest of the amusement park. The owners do not plan to rebuild.

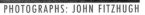

PHOTOGRAPHS: JOHN FITZHUGH

PHOTOGRAPH: TIM ISBELL

PHOTOGRAPH: JOHN FITZHUGH

THE GOLDEN FISHERMAN BILOXI

For many, the 15-foot Golden Fisherman is a symbol of Biloxi fishing heritage. It was unveiled in 1977 as part of an urban renewal effort in downtown Biloxi that eventually failed. In 2002, the sculpture, created by the late Harry Reeks, was moved to the foot of the Biloxi-Ocean Springs Bridge, where it cast its 20-foot-wide net toward the Biloxi Bay. Hurricane Katrina didn't wash the Golden Fisherman away but did topple him near his base on Point Cadet.

SEASHORE METHODIST ASSEMBLY BILOXI

Leggett Memorial United Methodist Church, located at the Seashore Methodist Assembly on Beach Boulevard in Biloxi, was barely a shell after Katrina and has since been bulldozed. Seashore, which was established in 1876, is used as an affordable retreat-conference center for local and regional educational, civic and religious gatherings.

Katrina hit the assembly hard. Van Hook Hall, which opened in 1911, still stands; two small motels, a bunk area for kids, and Casey Center, where classes are held, are in various stages of damage. The cafeteria has been used to feed relief workers. The future of Leggett Memorial and its role and location on Seashore Assembly are under discussion.

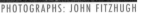

CHIMNEYS RESTAURANT
GULFPORT

The 1900s Queen Anne house was renovated in 1999 to become the Chimneys, a restaurant owned by Peter and Dix Nord, who moved from the Long Beach Harbor site to the house on Gulfport's Beach Boulevard. The work the Nords put into the house was cited in 2004 by the Gulfport Downtown Association as a significant contribution to revitalizing the area. Chimneys was a popular fine dining restaurant known for seafood dishes and a spectacular view of the Mississippi Sound. The turn-of-the-last-century house was destroyed Aug. 29, 2005, by Hurricane Katrina. The Nords are undecided about their plans.

THE DANTZLER HOUSE
BILOXI

The Dantzler House was built in the early 1850s. It was many things during its history, from a fine home for cotton planters and lumber magnates to a Catholic school to the headquarters of the Biloxi Tricentennial Commission. The most recent plan for the Historic Register house at 1042 Beach Blvd. was to be the Biloxi Mardi Gras Museum. Many carnival artifacts were there in storage as exhibits were planned. The museum was to open in 2006. Katrina claimed the Mardi Gras paraphernalia and the house, too. The only thing saved from the Dantzler House was eight stained-glass windows found in the middle of a pile of rubble.

PHOTOGRAPHS: JOHN FITZHUGH

BEACHWALK CONDOMINIUMS
LONG BEACH

In June, the second phase of the Beachwalk Condominiums in Long Beach was nearly finished. All that was left to do before Katrina was to put in the gates. In September, only the sign for Beachwalk Condominiums stood. The developer said he found his FEMA-approved breakaway walls from the bottom-floor garages about a block away.

77

PHOTOGRAPH: TIM ISBELL

PHOTOGRAPH: JOHN FITZHUGH

FIRST BAPTIST CHURCH
GULFPORT

First Baptist Church of Gulfport was established two years before the port became an official city. In 1896, the first congregation met in a private home before erecting its first building near the train depot at the center of town. In its current location, First Baptist occupies 1½ downtown blocks and fronts on U.S. 90. The sanctuary steeple still stands tall, but the worship center itself has no walls and much of the roof is gone. The first floors of its administration, activity and three educational buildings are gutted and other floors damaged. The church plans to move north of Interstate 10.

WHITE CAP
SEAFOOD RESTAURANT
GULFPORT

The White Cap Seafood Restaurant, located at the south end of the Gulfport Small Craft Harbor, offered diners a clear view of the harbor and port ships. Fresh Mississippi Sound and Gulf shrimp were a specialty, as were the pressed, dressed po-boys. One of the oldest restaurants in the state, the White Cap had been around in one form or another since 1929. Hurricane Katrina destroyed the iconic eatery, but owners say they will rebuild.

PHOTOGRAPH: CARA OWSLEY

PHOTOGRAPH: JOHN FITZHUGH

PHOTOGRAPH: JOHN FITZHUGH

PHOTOGRAPH: DAVID PURDY

Lynn Meadows Discovery Center, Mississippi's only children's museum when it opened in 1998, is nestled among ancient oaks in a vintage 1915 building that began as Mississippi City School. The neighborhood was eventually incorporated by Gulfport and the school became obsolete. The center was named one of the country's top 50 children's museums.

A 5-foot surge from Hurricane Katrina swept through the first floor of the school, but the second floor is usable as the staff rebuilds.

GRASS LAWN
GULFPORT

Grass Lawn, built in 1836 as a summer home for a Port Gibson surgeon, was thought to be the second-oldest house in Gulfport. Made of cypress and the sturdy yellow pine that used to grow in South Mississippi's ancient forests, it was of "pegged" construction. But, despite its solid frame, Katrina destroyed what nearly two centuries of other storms could not. Grass Lawn is now rubble. Every piece of wood that can be identified as Grass Lawn is being saved and the future of the site is under discussion.

PHOTOGRAPH: TIM ISBELL

PHOTOGRAPH: JOHN FITZHUGH

PHOTOGRAPH: JOHN FITZHUGH

PHOTOGRAPH: DAVID PURDY

BILOXI - OCEAN SPRINGS BRIDGE

The first bridge taking people from Biloxi to Ocean Springs was a toll span that opened in 1930 and was dedicated as the nation's longest World War I monument, all 4,200 feet of it. After 32 years, though, the two-laner was turned into a fishing pier and replaced with a new bridge just to the south of it. That bridge, the one claimed by Katrina, opened in May 1962 with a $7 million price tag, and was repaired seven years later after Camille. The new bridge is tentatively scheduled to be finished March 2008.

GULFPORT SMALL CRAFT HARBOR

Howard Rabone of Long Beach walks along one of the misty piers at the Gulfport Small Craft Harbor in December 2000, after checking on his boat. After Gulfport officially became a city in 1898, it was not long before pleasure boats joined the working boats, and a yacht club and pavilion social center was in place by 1903. After Hurricane Katrina, no one could walk down the piers, which the city plans to rebuild.

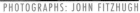

PHOTOGRAPHS: JOHN FITZHUGH

PHOTOGRAPH: CARA OWSLEY

PHOTOGRAPH: JOHN FITZHUGH

BROADWATER RESORT BILOXI

The Broadwater Marina is located directly across U.S. 90 from the former Broadwater Resort, a famous Coast hotel property that played host to movie stars and presidents. It later also became the home for the President Casino. Hurricane Katrina displaced the President's gambling barge. Before Katrina, the casino barge had been sold to Silver Slipper Casino Venture LLC. But the hurricane's tidal surge washed the barge from its moorings and smashed it into the Biloxi Beachfront Hotel about a half mile to the west. A new casino resort will be built at the Broadwater site.

BROADWATER MARINA
BILOXI

The Broadwater Beach Marina opened in 1965 with a price tag of $3.5 million. T.M. Dorset Jr., who designed this marina for Dorothy Brown with attractive, scalloped slip covers of pre-stressed steel-reinforced concrete, called it "his baby." Built 15 feet high, it was considered hurricane proof at the time and was home to many charter and private boats. It survived Camille and others, but not Katrina.

PHOTOGRAPH: TIM ISBELL

PHOTOGRAPH: JOHN FITZHUGH

PHOTOGRAPH: JOHN FITZHUGH

141 DAVIS AVENUE
PASS CHRISTIAN

Six decades after Micah Keel's great-grandfather operated Marquez & Keel Garage at 141 Davis Ave., Keel opened a business in the same place, whose history includes President Woodrow Wilson buying an ice cream cone there in 1914. He and his partner, Robert Padilla, restored the building in 2003 and opened Keel & Padilla, a financial consulting service for First Capital Management and Insurance. Attempts to locate the business partners since the storm were unsuccessful.

PHOTOGRAPH: JOHN FITZHUGH

PHOTOGRAPH COURTESY OF THE KEEL FAMILY

POINT CADET
BILOXI

Point Cadet, the eastern tip of Biloxi's peninsula, was once mostly woods until the late 1800s. With the coming of the seafood factories, it became home to the backbone workers who caught or processed the oysters and shrimp, from the Slavonians and French to the more recent Vietnamese. Not all the trees were cut down for fisherman's cottages, as this view of First and Maple streets shows. The tree canopy was so thick that it hid many roofs, as the post-Katrina panorama proves.

PHOTOGRAPHS: JOHN FITZHUGH

87

MARINE LIFE OCEANARIUM GULFPORT

Marine Life Oceanarium opened a half-century ago in the Gulfport Harbor, offering marine shows and tanks of interesting sea life. After Katrina, the dolphins were sent to Atlantis Resort in the Bahamas and the sea lions, birds and other animals that survived are being cared for in marine parks and zoos in Florida, Georgia, and Tennessee. "We are like so many other people on the Coast, working with our insurance company, trying to get property cleared up, and trying to figure out the future," said Marine Life president David Lion.

PHOTOGRAPH: DAVID PURDY

PHOTOGRAPH: JOHN FITZHUGH

PHOTOGRAPH: DAVID PURDY

HOBNOB CAFÉ
BILOXI

The HobNob Café, at 122-A Lameuse St. in Biloxi, featured lunch specials, special events and specialty baking on the side. Katrina destroyed all that was Pirates Alley, where the HobNob was located in Biloxi's historic The Fisherman's Cottage. The restaurant owners were Pauline, Lou and Gale Dean, who are now out of the restaurant business.

PHOTOGRAPH: KAT BERGERON

PHOTOGRAPH: JOHN FITZHUGH

WHITE HALL
PASS CHRISTIAN

Prentiss and Dee Havens renovated 1024 West Beach Blvd. in Pass Christian and often opened it for home tours and fund-raising parties. In fact, the Colonial Revival home called White Hall, built about 1885, was among the most toured homes for the past decade. Nine months ago, the Havenses sold to a woman who owns other large houses across the country, and as is often the tradition in the Pass for these nonpermanent residents, ownership names are closely guarded. After Katrina, the Havenses called the new owners with the sad news that White Hall was gone.

PHOTOGRAPH: VERNON MATTHEWS

TRINITY EPISCOPAL CHURCH PASS CHRISTIAN

Organized in 1849, Trinity Episcopal Church in Pass Christian was rebuilt after Hurricane Camille. It became a symbol of renewal. The sanctuary was almost 14 feet above sea level and the Katrina high-water mark is 22 feet above that. The roof and enough of the structure and floor remain that parishioners put up plywood and plastic to hold services there. Trinity will be rebuilt in the Carpenter Gothic style with four buildings and a central plaza that includes an open air chapel.

MISSISSIPPI CITY METHODIST CHURCH GULFPORT

Mississippi City United Methodist, which was founded somewhere around 1840, had 285 members before Hurricane Katrina washed ashore. In addition to sweeping out its sanctuary, located at 219 Courthouse Road in Gulfport, Katrina caused at least 50 of the church's members to move. Two crosses and a bell from the original church survived the storm. The sanctuary will be restored and a new fellowship hall built.

THE SEBASTES
BILOXI

The Taconis named the 36-foot sea skiff, one of the last wooden lapstrakes built by Chris Craft in 1959, Sebastes for *sebastes marinus*, or ocean red fish. Biloxian August Taconi Sr. bought it in the 1970s to begin a second career as a charter boat captain. As Katrina approached, his son Augie headed the Sebastes to safer waters, as most did on the Coast. He settled in Parker's Landing in Woolmarket and didn't get home for two days. When his dad asked about the boat, Augie told him it was "still up there." "I didn't lie. I just didn't give the condition," Augie said, "and he didn't ask." Two weeks later, just shy of 85, the elder Taconi died. "The boat had lived a good life, like my dad."

PHOTOGRAPHS COURTESY OF AUGUST TACONI JR.

PHOTOGRAPH: KEVIN COOPER

PHOTOGRAPH: JOHN FITZHUGH

LIGHTHOUSE PIER
BILOXI

A rare snow coated the Biloxi Lighthouse Pier in 1996. The pier and the lighthouse itself are at the foot of Porter Avenue. Katrina zapped one of the Coast's favorite and most visible piers. The city says it will rebuild the Biloxi Lighthouse Pier better and stronger. A pier on that site dates to the 1860s.

LONG BEACH OAKS

The Long Beach Oaks neighborhood is bordered on the right by Russell Avenue. Katrina left little for Long Beach residents to search through, not even at The Sleep Inn (far left). Long Beach, incorporated 100 years ago, had much of its homes and buildings between the beach and railroad, sometimes beyond, destroyed.

PHOTOGRAPH COURTESY OF LYNN CRAIG, AIA, RIBA, CLEMSON UNIVERSITY

PHOTOGRAPH COURTESY OF USGS

BEACH BOULEVARD SIGNS
GULFPORT - BILOXI

Sometimes Katrina took or wrecked signs on Beach Boulevard, the official U.S. 90 in Harrison County. Sometimes, she left the signs and wrecked the buildings they advertised. To the left is a section of Gulfport just east of Tegarden Road, where a business mix brought diners, sleepers, partiers, and shoppers. Below is a section of the Biloxi Strip, west of Rodenberg Avenue. It was developed in the mid-20th century as a tourist area for family entertainment, nightclubs and lodging.

PHOTOGRAPHS: JOHN FITZHUGH

TIGRES SUPPER CLUB
PASS CHRISTIAN

Tigre's opened on West Second in 2000, after Pass business partners Thomas Genin and Victor Pickich turned 21. They had to wait until they were old enough for a liquor license. The irony of Katrina taking their popular fine-dining restaurant is that a hurricane lured them toward restaurants. When in high school, someone from Chef Emeril Lagasse's staff evacuated to a cousin's house when a storm threatened New Orleans, and as Pickich said, "The next thing we knew we were at Emeril's' back door." After high school graduation, they attended separate culinary academies, then opened in the Pass. Four months after Katrina, they opened Tigre's Supper Club in The Oaks, a posh Pass neighborhood. They're looking for Coast property to rebuild.

PHOTOGRAPH: JAMES EDWARD BATES

PHOTOGRAPH: JOHN FITZHUGH

PHOTOGRAPH: JOHN FITZHUGH

PHOTOGRAPH COURTESY OF BOURDIN FAMILY

BOURDIN BUILDING
PASS CHRISTIAN

The Bourdin property at 104 Market St. in downtown Pass Christian was home to Adolph Bourdin Air Conditioning & Heating as well as other businesses. Today the company remains a family business. Adolph died in 1975, knowing his tradesmen skills had worn off on son Robert, and then onto the next generation. The building was lost in Katrina.

PHOTOGRAPHS COURTESY OF BUZZY BOLTON

BOLTON HOUSE
BILOXI

The bungalow at 1084 Beach Blvd. in Biloxi was built in 1920 by Dr. Walter T. Bolton. The Bolton House remained in the family several generations before Katrina. What the Boltons had was a family compound, and through the years, assorted family members lived in the four structures on the land that stretched from the beach road to Bolton Lane. Katrina swept it away, including 1084. All that remains is a set of steps.

PHOTOGRAPH: BETH MUSGRAVE

PHOTOGRAPH: JOHN FITZHUGH

FOUNTAIN PARK
D'IBERVILLE

The new marine education center and expanded Fountain Pier included a series of boardwalks and a two-story educational pavilion built by the city with Tidelands Funds, collected by the state primarily from leases to casinos. City officials are saddened by the Katrina losses there, especially of a half-dozen 300-year-old oak trees dating to the landing of the French. As for the man-made part, "We will rebuild," said Mayor Rusty Quave.

PHOTOGRAPH: DAVID PURDY

PHOTOGRAPH: JOHN FITZHUGH

SNEIRSON HOME
PASS CHRISTIAN

Four months before Katrina, Marilyn and Bill Sneirson decided they would sell their New Jersey house and retire on the Coast to be closer to their New Orleans daughter. They bought the 1850s Colonial Revival, with its terrazzo-floored porch, that Cynthia Hammond had often opened to home tours. The Sneirsons began furnishing it in June and Katrina took everything, price tags and all. "We were totally charmed by the town," he said. "We're hoping to rebuild, applying super modern updated construction techniques to create something like it used to look."

PHOTOGRAPH: DAVID PURDY

PHOTOGRAPH: JOHN FITZHUGH

THE DENTON HOUSE
BILOXI

The Denton House on Beach Boulevard in Biloxi was a Colonial Revival built around 1910, probably as a summer home for a New Orleans lumber businessman named Capt. John Smith. The home's owners were the late Will Denton, a colorful Biloxi attorney, and his wife Lucy, who is known for her civic activities. In 2001, both appeared — along with their house — in an episode of *If Walls Could Talk*, a popular program on the Home & Garden Television channel. Hurricane Katrina apparently lifted the house, moved it and then sent it crumbling to the ground.

ACADIAN VILLAGE
GULFPORT

Its size — just 40 units — is a hint that Acadian Village at 4710 West Beach Blvd. is one of the earlier condominium developments. Built in 1982, "It was quality, not quantity," said Jim Clark, president of the owner's association who lives in Georgia but grew up in Gulfport not far from where he would buy four condos. Acadian Village was meticulously maintained and had a beautiful location and old world charm." After Katrina, nothing higher than 10 inches remained of the 10 buildings, each with four condos, designed after New Orleans French architecture. No decision will be made on rebuilding until after the condo owners association meets.

PHOTOGRAPHS: JOHN FITZHUGH

101

MARIA PLACE
GULFPORT

Jim and Deborah Barnes came from Birmingham to buy investment property on the prospering Coast. When they saw Maria Place, they bought not only one of the homes for themselves but the two other 2,200 square-foot, New Orleans-Charleston style houses. The three were staggered for waterfront views from balconies, and by Aug. 29, 2005, one was still under construction. "They were beautiful, well-appointed houses, an awesome piece of property," said Debbie Gomila, the listing agent with Owen & Co. Real Estate who introduced the Barnes to the project at the corner of Maria Avenue and West Beach Boulevard. The Barnes have joined with Shoreline Development and an architect is designing four new homes for the site.

PHOTOGRAPH: CARA OWSLEY

PHOTOGRAPHS COURTESY OF T.J. MORAN

MORAN ART STUDIO
BILOXI

Joe Moran, a Biloxi boat builder-turned-artist, opened Moran Art Studio in the 1960s and moved it in 1970 to the Davis family homestead of his wife, Dorothy. The structure, originally a 1920s house and coffee warehouse, was near the south end of Porter Avenue, a location that served well as a studio-home. A burial mound found there became an archaeological curiosity. Even the Smithsonian Institution took note of Moran's artistic skills, which seem to run in the family, beginning with noted art potter George Ohr. After Hurricane Katrina, nothing remains of the studio. Some of Moran's originals were found 1½ blocks away. Losses include two of the family favorites, a night shrimping scene and the portrait of his wife. A George Ohr ceramic pot was found broken in two.

PHOTOGRAPH: JOHN FITZHUGH

MCDONALD'S SIGN
BILOXI

For more than four decades, Speedee loomed atop the McDonald's sign on 1644 Pass Road. The mascot on the original sign was a reminder of times when hamburgers were 15 cents and a soft drink was a nickel. When the sign went up in 1962, the owner was Stephen Dietz, who'd started the Biloxi franchise as a teen. Now it's owned by the McDonald's corporation, which says it is hoping to save the landmark.

WILLIAM CAREY COLLEGE
GULFPORT

William Carey College on the Coast's administration building was built in 1921 as part of Gulf Coast Military Academy. The10,738-square-foot Fairchild Hall, was gutted by Hurricane Katrina and condemned, along with every other building on campus except for the back four dormitories. The college plans to sell the property.

PHOTOGRAPHS: DREW TARTER

OLD BRICK HOUSE
BILOXI

The mid-1800s house of locally made brick is one of Biloxi's most important structures because it represents the period of the city's earliest substantial settlement. The front porch of the Old Brick House in Biloxi collapsed during Hurricane Katrina, but the structure will be saved.

PHOTOGRAPH: JOHN FITZHUGH

PHOTOGRAPH: JAMES EDWARD BATES

MIHOJEVICH HOME
BILOXI

Built circa 1926 as a small grocery, 130 Myrtle St. was converted into a house and fit well into the fisherman cottages on Biloxi's Point Cadet. After Katrina, owner Marguerite Mihojevich sold the vacant lot to a casino resort.

PHOTOGRAPHS COURTESY OF MARGEURITE MIHOJEVICH

HANS HOME
GULFPORT

1520 Hewes Ave., built in 1964, became John Hans dream house in 1996 for a high mortgage he says was worth it: "I could lay in my bed in the morning and look out and see Cat Island and the Gulfport Ship Channel and know what kind of day it would be." He will copy it when rebuilding.

PHOTOGRAPHS COURTESY OF JOHN HANS

UNION HOUSE
PASS CHRISTIAN

Family tradition says that Mary Saucier obliged Civil War Union soldiers who briefly occupied her house in1862 when they requested she play *The Bonnie Blue Flag*. Known locally as Union House, it was built about 1855. Jane and Dave Dennis, owners of Specialty Contractors, had a contract to buy the house before Katrina and closed in December after it was in shambles. The Dennises have salvaged the timber and brick to reuse. "We are still in the planning process, but as soon as it's practical, it's our intent to proceed with a mixed-use property that conforms to the spirit of the charette process and melds together the history of the property, new realistic building codes, and aesthetics."

PHOTOGRAPH: CARA OWSLEY

PHOTOGRAPH: JOHN FITZHUGH

BRECKENRIDGE HOME
PASS CHRISTIAN

Darryl and Amanda Breckenridge purchased their circa 1850 Creole cottage at 239 East Second St. in 1988. Although it was not one of the antebellum splendors in Pass Christian, its role as one of the charming homes that created an interesting mix of people and places is obvious. The house, whatever its history, was well built and didn't fall apart when 11 feet of Katrina surge flooded to the inside crown moulding and swept it off its foundation. The attic, miraculously, stayed dry.

SHARKHEADS GIFT SHOP BILOXI

The giant 30-foot shark that gave Sharkheads Gift Shop its name was a popular place for tourists to shop and take pictures. The shocking pink building behind it on Beach Boulevard in Biloxi dispels the scariness of the scene. The shark head was made of fiberglass and foam material. Officials suspect it simply disintegrated when hit by Hurricane Katrina's tidal surge. The owners, the Pierotich family, say they will rebuild – with a new shark head.

PHOTOGRAPH: TIM ISBELL

PHOTOGRAPH: JOHN FITZHUGH

CHATEAU DE LA MER GULFPORT

In 1981, drivers on Beach Boulevard in Gulfport watched with fascination as huge cranes lifted rectangular, modular units into the air and set them on a large concrete pier foundation. The end result was Chateau de La Mer, a resort condominium at the corner of Cowan-Lorraine Road. It was host to snowbirds and year-round residents. Hurricane Katrina destroyed some units but left others standing on their cement foundations, basically inaccessible and unstable. The land at U.S. 90 and Cowan Road is now for sale.

BOGGSDALE HOME
LONG BEACH

Boggsdale is legendary but as real as the family that slowly built a compound of 11 homes, large and small but always seaside restful. "This is not a Kennedy compound built with money," said Claire Morrison, who grew up there and built a home of her own. "Boggsdale was built with love and sweat and tears." In 1875, Georgian artist and writer Robert Boggs and wife Eliza Jane bought seven acres at what would become Long Beach. "My children all were planning on retiring early and living the good life. Now they have to start over again, including myself at age 90."

PHOTOGRAPHS: JOHN FITZHUGH

PHOTOGRAPHS: JOHN FITZHUGH

MCELROY'S SEAFOOD RESTAURANT BILOXI

The Harbor House, with such popular items as stuffed flounder and po-boys, was opened in 1974 by Mickey McElroy and his parents. The family business expanded four times and had 85 employees before Katrina. Two years ago, the family opened McElroy's on the Bayou in Ocean Springs, which received 7 feet of water but reopened by Christmas. As for Harbor House, "onward and upward. Why would there be anything else but to reopen?" said Mickey McElroy.

FRIENDSHIP OAK
LONG BEACH

Among the first questions of callers to the newspaper after a hurricane: "Is Friendship Oak ok?" The tree, thought to be at least 500 years old, is a symbol of friendship and durability and stands on the University of Southern Mississippi Gulf Coast Campus in Long Beach. The tree survived but the fate of the USM campus, which had $15.5 million in damage at that site is unknown until the State College Board rules.

PHOTOGRAPHS: TIM ISBELL

"It turned out I was the silly one."

BY KAT BERGERON

A blue pirogue, wedged in the front doorway, kept the diminutive Yvonne Davis Scott from drowning.

At less than 5 feet tall and less than 100 pounds, the 91-year-old Pascagoula native struggled to stay afloat inside her 1920s home as Katrina's water reached her chin. Slippery muck and her uncontrollable floatability made standing impossible.

When a pirogue miraculously floated down the waterway that was once the street to 710 Ford Ave., a granddaughter swam out to grab it.

The back of the homemade, flat-bottom skiff wouldn't go through the front door, but enough fit inside to allow Yvonne's son to hoist her into the pirogue. There she sat, survival instincts revved, as she held an old gray crocheted purse atop her head.

As the water rose, 10 others bobbed safely inside the house, avoiding furniture floaters. When it became obvious Katrina was like no other storm, they all had waded to Yvonne's "safe" house, the one that never flooded. This time, water from the sound and bayous converged in the neighborhood east of downtown Pascagoula.

As she watched from the pirogue, a surreal nightmare unfolded. Her son's knuckles grew white as he clung to the side of the blue skiff so it would not unwedge from the doorjamb and float into the rushing water topped with white caps.

Then a horrible realization struck him: What if the water rose higher than the ceiling? The skiff would become a death trap.

"I was ready to push my mother and the boat out into the storm rather than let her drown inside," said Harold "Scotty" B. Scott Jr. "But I didn't have to."

The water nightmare lasted four hours, maybe more, maybe less. Here, it rose more steadily than it surged, and that, combined with daylight to see by, is why the Scott family can celebrate survival.

Yvonne is known for remarkable health (does yoga, walks miles and takes no medicine), for remarkable luck (parking and last-minute appointments magically appear) and for a strong faith (Mass every morning). Her crossword-a-day mind is sharp, her memory intact, except for the hours Katrina stole.

"I don't remember praying during the storm, but I've done plenty since," she said.

Yvonne had decided to ride out the storm alone in the house she's lived in 71 years. It was built in the 1920s by her father-in-law. She and her late postmaster husband raised six children there. Extended family live nearby, including son Scotty next door.

At least a dozen of the Scotts lost homes to Katrina. Hers stands but with an uncertain future. Was the water contaminated from nearby industry? Can she afford to raise it higher? She did not have flood insurance.

Yvonne Scott is not a person of big regrets, but she does have one. She didn't think to ask her family to save the blue pirogue. When no one claimed it, the skiff was hauled away with so much other storm debris.

"This house has never flooded before, not even during Camille," she said. "I had neighbors who called to say Pascagoula was evacuating. I said that was the silliest thing I'd ever heard. It turned out I was the silly one."

JACKSON COUNTY

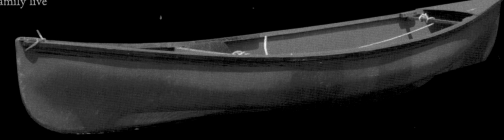

PHOTOGRAPH COURTESY OF THE TILLMAN FAMILY

PHOTOGRAPH: JOHN FITZHUGH

BOSIO HOME PASCAGOULA

The Bosio house at 1025 Beach Blvd. in Pascagoula was a mixture of the old and the new, though it was difficult to tell which was which. It attracted photographers after Katrina because of the oddity of one addition still standing, a section that housed Dr. Bruner Bosio's study. The land has since been bulldozed.

The 19th-century, waterfront McFaul House was a Pascagoula landmark when the Bosios bought it from the McFaul-Rigby family, who built and owned it for a century. The house began a new chapter when the Bosios moved in 1988. With four children to raise there, the family added "wings" but kept the 2,000-square-foot main house intact and modernized with 19th-century charm in mind.

ALEXANDER HOUSE
ST. MARTIN

The home at 15604 Rue Dauphin at Langley Point was built by Joe Alexander, a general contractor known for carpentry magic. The speculation house was a showpiece of his talents. He, wife Mary and the kids moved in in 1989, fell in love with the house and never sold it.

PHOTOGRAPHS COURTESY OF THE ALEXANDER FAMILY

OCEAN SPRINGS SEAFOOD

The Fayard family started Ocean Springs Seafood in 1948 on Front Beach Boulevard. The 1.18 acres was the site of a seafood business even before Elfine Fayard bought it more than a half century ago to operate with her son Earl Fayard Sr. It has remained a three-generation family business. Future plans are uncertain.

PHOTOGRAPH: SEAN LOFTIN

PHOTOGRAPH: JOHN FITZHUGH

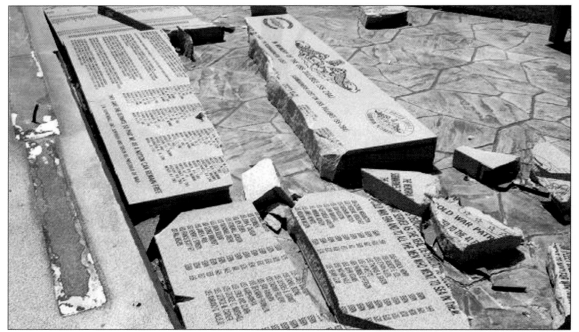

MISSISSIPPI SUBMARINE MEMORIAL
OCEAN SPRINGS

Completed in 2003, the Mississippi Submarine Memorial was dedicated to all who have served and died on U.S. submarines, as well as those who died in 1944 on the USS Tullibee, torpedoed in the Pacific. The memorial was 15 feet long and 6 feet high and nestled in the Vietnam War Veterans' Memorial Park. It will be rebuilt with thicker granite and heavier dowels for wind resistance.

PHOTOGRAPHS COURTESY OF HERB EDMONDS

EGAN COTTAGE
OCEAN SPRINGS

Egan Cottage at 314 Jackson St. is named after the Irish immigrant who built the house in the 1860s. He was master at the steamboat wharf, postmaster, justice of the peace and bar proprietor. The cottage owners, Ray and Maureen Hudachek, have hired an architect to replicate the house. "It was not one of the majestic houses but a homey house in 1963 when we found it," she said. "We don't want to go anywhere else."

PHOTOGRAPH: RAY L. BELLANDE

PHOTOGRAPH: JOHN FITZHUGH

SYKES HOME
PASCAGOULA

Johnny and Camille Sykes bought this colonial-style home on Beach Boulevard in Pascagoula after falling in love with the area. The roof of the Sykes house survived Katrina, though the rest of the house was destroyed. In 1988, the Sykes bought waterfront property on Beach Boulevard, just west of the public beach. Soon a local contractor, Irby Tillman, began work on a two-story colonial-style home. Before the house was finished, Tillman told Sykes the roof was specially made, reinforced with steel beams inside the front columns. A perfect foe for hurricane-force winds, he believed. "When she comes," Tillman told Sykes, "we won't lose the roof." And they didn't.

PHOTOGRAPH COURTESY OF THE TILLMAN FAMILY

PHOTOGRAPH: JOHN FITZHUGH

PHOTOGRAPH: TIM ISBELL

PHOTOGRAPH: JOHN FITZHUGH

LOTT HOME PASCAGOULA

A young Trent Lott rode his bike along Beach Boulevard and always stopped at his favorite spot and dreamed of owning the 1854 Creole-style house. That happened in 1984 when he was in his 40s and the congressional minority whip. Katrina took it all and the now-U.S. senator is among those with flood insurance but not enough to rebuild. He is suing the insurance company to set a precedent for use of homeowners' policies.

VILLA ROSA
OCEAN SPRINGS

Ross and Sharon Dodds' home at 505 Front Beach Drive in Ocean Springs, Villa Rosa, was thought to be built in the 1860s by Italian boat builder and brick-yard operator Louis E. Dolbear. It had in every room the artistic touch of its last owner. Sharon Dodd, an Ocean Springs artist, had painted trompe l'oeil screens and floors, even created mosaic floors from local pottery shards after she and her botanist husband renovated the vine-covered Italianate-style house on Front Beach. They furnished it in French and Italian antiques and showcased art from Europe, New Orleans and the Coast.

The Dodds consider themselves luckier than many because they were renovating a smaller house three blocks away that received little hurricane damage. "We plan to press on and remember the grand times on Front Beach. We have wonderful memories of that house."

PHOTOGRAPHS: JOHN FITZHUGH

PHOTOGRAPHS: JOHN FITZHUGH

FORT MAUREPAS
OCEAN SPRINGS

Fort Maurepas is the re-creation of one of the original settlements in South Mississippi. Local historians would don period clothing to help tell the story of the area. The main structure and most of the fencing of Fort Maurepas in Ocean Springs was leveled by Hurricane Katrina, though the roof did stay somewhat intact. Fort Maurepas is the heart of French Colonial history on the Mississippi Coast. It was the first fort, so many argue it was the first capital of the vast Louisiana Territory. A replica of the fort was built in the 1980s on Front Beach Boulevard The original fort was constructed in 1699 by Iberville, leader of the land-claiming expedition of King Louis XIV of France. The French later moved their headquarters to Mobile, then to present-day Biloxi, then permanently to New Orleans. The replica was conceived in the 1970s by founders of the 1699 Historical Committee, which hosts a colorful "Iberville Landing" pageant each spring.

LAWLER HOME
OCEAN SPRINGS

Shannon and Jessica Lawler flew from California in 2003 to check housing prospects as they prepared to move to a new job at Northrop Grumman. "What we wanted are the two things you can't have in California: land and water," Lawler said. "As soon as we saw 232 Lover's Lane, we looked at each other and said to the Realtor, 'I want this house even if it is all pink inside.'" It was.

The Lawlers immediately changed color schemes and started a love affair with Lover's Lane, with the neighbors, the views, and a history that links it to early French settlement. They plan to rebuild 20 feet above sea level but what will they call the new house? Lawler laughed: "We're thinking of either Stubbornness or Stupidity."

PHOTOGRAPHS COURTESY OF SHANNON LAWLER

PHOTOGRAPHS COURTESY OF DR. THOMAS SEGLIO

SEGLIO HOME
OCEAN SPRINGS

The expansive windows of the Seglio home at 303 Front Beach Drive in Ocean Springs displayed its waterfront views. The Dr. Thomas Seglio family of Ocean Springs plans to rebuild after Katrina took everything. Seglio and his wife, Angelina, bought their Mediterranean-style house for its view of Deer Island and its neighborhood feel. Clay tiles topped the 4,500-square-foot house and the oak trees were "breathtaking," in the opinion of the Seglios. They had the best view of holiday fireworks shows, to boot. "The storm left us with only two side chairs out of a dining room set that was part of a wedding gift," said Angelina Seglio, a respiratory nurse whose husband is an emergency room director. "Our plans are to eventually rebuild," she said. "We're fighters. We're not going to let the storm push us around. We've fallen in love with the Gulf Coast. It's a magical place."

MARTIN HOME
OCEAN SPRINGS

Hurricane Katrina left the two oaks that framed Alice and Gay Martin's home in Ocean Springs, but little else. Alice Martin's family settled at 545 Front Beach Blvd. 65 years ago into an interesting raised cottage built in 1923. The age is deceptive because the Ocean Springs house was rebuilt on a basement that dated to an 1880s house destroyed by fire. The stucco-frame house overlooking Deer Island had 11-foot ceilings, a wraparound porch and was built with huge timbers. Heart of pine, cypress and stucco were used in construction. After Katrina leveled the house, she and husband Gay spent 2½ hours in a giant cedar tree, where they had floated on part of the roof.

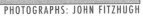

PHOTOGRAPHS: JOHN FITZHUGH

PHOTOGRAPH: RAY L. BELLANDE

NOBLIN HOME
OCEAN SPRINGS

The concrete steps at 101 Ashley Place — 17 of them that put this house 18.5 feet above sea level — lived up to construction workers' predictions that they would withstand storms. Originally, the staircase was wooden but when the family of orthopedic surgeon Jeff Noblin moved into the 1995, 3,500 square foot house in 2002, they had new steps constructed. The Noblins say they will rebuild, but they don't know yet if they'll use the same steps.

PHOTOGRAPH: JOHN FITZHUGH

BELLE FONTAINE BEACH

Katrina left stilts to nowhere and an occasional washed-out house at Belle Fontaine. In French, the name Belle Fontaine translates as a beautiful spring or beautiful fountain. Belle Fontaine is one of the few Mississippi Coast beach fronts with most houses raised high on stilts, much like those found on the Alabama and Florida coasts. There are records that families lived on Belle Fontaine as early as the 1770s. The graceful, raised homes did not impress Hurricane Katrina. The massive storm surge blasted the homes off their stilts, leaving nothing but the foundations as testimony to their existence.

PHOTOGRAPH: JOHN FITZHUGH

PHOTOGRAPH: DAVID PURDY

The image at the immediate left was taken less than two months before Katrina and captures the waterfront view of 6317 West Belle Fontaine Beach Rd. in Jackson County. The hurricane-damaged lot there was recently bought sight unseen by a Chicago businessman, Mike Ruter, who wants to build a vacation home. Ruter thought the waterfront property in Florida and Alabama was too pricey for him, so he looked to the west. "I don't know what I was expecting when I came to Mississippi, but what I saw wasn't what I was expecting," Ruter said. "The landscape and oak trees are incredible."

PHOTOGRAPH: RAY L. BELLANDE

PHOTOGRAPH: JOHN FITZHUGH

ASHLEY HOME
SHEARWATER COMPOUND
OCEAN SPRINGS

The Andersons were the third owners of 102-C Shearwater, and this house, built in 1833, was there when they bought the 24 acres for $1,500 in 1918. George Anderson didn't want his wife to chose it, leery of living close to the water with storms, but she thought it a great place to encourage the artistic muses of their children. Called The Front House, or "Mamma and Daddy's House," it was, "a wonderful house for gatherings" as Peter Anderson, the potter who started Shearwater, would say. He was the "Daddy" because after he married, his parents let him restore the house and that's where Peter's four children grew up. The owners are his daughter, Marjorie Ashley, and her husband James, who contemplate putting a small cottage there so descendants will have a place to come.

PICKARD HOME
SHEARWATER COMPOUND

Mary Pickard, one of Walter Anderson's daughters, grew up on the family compound at 102-D Shearwater. "Shearwater was a place where we were very, very close to the natural world," she said, "and that's what makes it hard now with the trees being gone and the bareness of the earth, which of course will heal in time." Eventually she and former husband, architect Edward Earl Pickard, built a house there with a design that reflected dominate coastal architecture.

They started in 1979 but didn't move in until 1986 because he was teaching architecture elsewhere. Pickard is undecided whether she will rebuild but is contemplating a small cottage.

PHOTOGRAPH: RAY L. BELLANDE

PHOTOGRAPH: JOHN FITZHUGH

PHOTOGRAPH: RAY L. BELLANDE

PHOTOGRAPH: JOHN FITZHUGH

JIM ANDERSON HOME
SHEARWATER COMPOUND
OCEAN SPRINGS

The Shearwater family compound includes Shearwater Pottery, named after the local black-and-white skimmer. Katrina destroyed or badly damaged 15 of the 17 houses and buildings, including the quaint showroom. A pilot preservation program stabilized the historic Walter Anderson Cottage, but restoration monies for much of the rest are questionable because the Andersons run a for-profit pottery. This was the home of potter Jim Anderson, who built the house in 1999 and who hopes to rebuild, so he again can throw clay on a potter's wheel.

LAKE MARS PIER
JACKSON COUNTY

When Tropical Storm Cindy swept through, she claimed the end of Lake Mars Pier and a lot of its night lighting. The popular pier is near Gulf Park Estates and the county had completed the last repairs the Friday before Katrina. Plans are to rebuild.

PHOTOGRAPHS: JOHN FITZHUGH

CROSBY HOME
OCEAN SPRINGS

When Keith and Patti Crosby built their dream home on the water in Ocean Springs' Gulf Park Estates in 1999, they called it an oasis, reflected in palm trees and beautiful landscaping. Hurricane Katrina destroyed the home, leaving only a slab of the 2,400-square-foot home at 9525 Seacliff Blvd. "We will rebuild, stronger, higher and smaller," said Patti Crosby. "It has such a beautiful view."

PHOTOGRAPHS COURTESY OF PATTI CROSBY

PHOTOGRAPH: RAY L. BELLANDE

WELDON HOME
OCEAN SPRINGS

Dr. John Weldon and his wife Germaine enjoyed their 1905 house at 207 Washington Ave. because it was within walking distance to historic downtown Ocean Springs and because they could stand on their screened front porch and talk to passersby. It was one of those kinds of neighborhoods. "It's not just the loss of the house but the loss of the neighborhood," said Dr. Weldon. "It was a very comfortable house, a combination of the old and new." Built as a New Orleans escape, the cottage became theirs in 1988, and they moved in after an addition was complete in 1990. That's where the "old and new" came in. "We're going to keep the land for now," he said, "and are strongly considering building back."

PHOTOGRAPH: JOHN FITZHUGH

PHOTOGRAPH COURTESY OF LISA WAGONER

PHOTOGRAPH: RAY L. BELLANDE

PHOTOGRAPH: JOHN FITZHUGH

WAGONER HOME
OCEAN SPRINGS

Fifteen years ago, Marty and Lisa Wagoner bought the Creole cottage at 409 East Beach Drive, top left, built in 1973 to look the old style, because "it was just a house that spoke to you." Then they bought the little cottage next door, which they were told was built after Camille by the American Red Cross for an elderly woman who'd lost her house. Katrina took both cottages adjoined with a courtyard. In July, the Wagoners, who own a financial consulting firm, hope to move into the first 758-square-foot house built by the local Katrina Cottage Group.

NORTHROP GRUMMAN SHIP SYSTEMS PASCAGOULA

Northrop Grumman's Ship Systems has a new motto since Katrina, "We build ships...nothing stands in our way." The proof is that the Pascagoula shipyard, opened in 1938 by Alabama industrialist Robert I. Ingalls, was up to 95 percent post-Katrina capacity in late March, 2006, which represents about 11,500 workers.

"The thing we've been most impressed with is people who showed up every day wanting to work. Someone who might have been a welder was pushing a broom to clear debris or shoveling mud," said Bill Glenn of the public relations office.

These photos are of the West Bank, where much work on Navy and Coast Guard contracts is done. The computer center and human resource buildings were destroyed in Katrina, along with more than 200 vehicles. With more than 6 feet of water, crane engines were affected by salt water.

CHEVRON REFINERY PASCAGOULA

Hurricane Georges in 1998 whacked the Chevron refinery, and it was out of commission for three months. When it reopened, there was a 20-foot levy to protect it. "The levy worked well and there was little flooding in the refinery," said Chevron spokesman Steve Renfroe, following Katrina. "It was mostly wind damage to cooling towers and wharf area. He said the refinery opened in six weeks.

PHOTOGRAPH: TIM ISBELL

PHOTOGRAPH: DAVID PURDY

PAQUETTE HOUSE
PASCAGOULA

Inventor J.J. Paquette of New Orleans built the unusual eight-angled, or octagonal, house in 1921, doing some of the work himself with family.

More recently, Norman and Carol Waddell lived at the Paquette House at 703 Washington Avenue for 32 years. It was even featured in the HGTV's *If Walls Could Talk*.

The Waddell's dream home underwent several renovations, including an octagonal screened porch. "It was a great place to raise a family, a dead-end street with 220 feet of waterfront for boating and canoeing," said Waddell, a retired shipyard engineer. They have relocated to Pensacola.

THE SULLIVAN HOUSE
OCEAN SPRINGS

In 1890, noted Chicago architect Louis H. Sullivan bought six acres in Ocean Springs. His brother and several friends bought acreage around him, creating a Chicago neighborhood. "Peace, peace and the joy of comrades" Sullivan wrote about where he built himself a house at 100 Holcomb Blvd. The "Dean of American Architects" used it as an escape for 20 years. The property was most recently owned by attorney Paul and Sylvia Minor.

PHOTOGRAPH: RAY L. BELLANDE

PHOTOGRAPH: JOHN FITZHUGH

139

PHOTOGRAPH: JOHN FITZHUGH

PHOTOGRAPH: JOHN FITZHUGH

SHEEHAN HOME
OCEAN SPRINGS

When Pat and Sue Sheehan bought the century-old Ocean Springs cottage at 420 Martin Ave. in 1983, they heard it originally sat on the beach but was moved in 1905. The cottage underwent updates, which the Sheehans undid to return it to an 1880s house. "We have a dearth of historical houses now and this one is salvageable," said attorney Pat Sheehan. "It's a question of whether its cost effective."

PHOTOGRAPH: RAY L. BELLANDE

ST. JUDE HOME
ST. MARTIN

Cathie Smith was eating in Leakesville when she heard she and her husband won the St. Jude house at 6204 Ascott Drive. The house was valued at $250,000 and the Smiths borrowed the money to pay $90,000 in taxes, thinking "it was still a steal. You know the saying, 'Everyone has a moment of fame.' …now it's over and we will go back to Leakesville and try and rebuild."

PHOTOGRAPH COURTESY OF CATHIE SMITH

OCEAN SPRINGS
YACHT CLUB

The 150-member club moved to Plumbers Point in 1976, next to the U.S. 90 Bridge because the Front Beach site is great to teach children to swim and sail and to appease the social and boating muse of adults. Unique among Coast clubs, this one allowed watching a regatta from the clubhouse. It will be rebuilt.

PHOTOGRAPH: JOHN FITZHUGH

PHOTOGRAPH: RAY L. BELLANDE

ROBOHM HOME
OCEAN SPRINGS

Natalie and Donald Robohm spent three years building their Frank Lloyd Wright-inspired house, and with hurricanes in mind, created a surge protector in the guise of a front patio. The idea worked because, although washed out, the house stood. With insurance money for repairs, Robohm, who runs an aquaculture farm, searched for a contractor and got a second Katrina whammy when no contractor he contacted would undertake the extensive restoration. It was bulldozed in mid-March.

PHOTOGRAPH: JOHN FITZHUGH

PHOTOGRAPH: RAY L. BELLANDE

PHOTOGRAPH: JOHN FITZHUGH

WHITE HOME
OCEAN SPRINGS

In love with Lover's Lane, attorney Jeff and Kari White built in 1997 at 235 Lover's Lane. As Katrina approached, they video-taped, then left the camera behind and had to double back, a good move since everything disappeared. "We're not going to build back there," she said. "Some things about Lover's Lane I will miss, but I won't miss the storm season."

PHOTOGRAPH: RAY L. BELLANDE

TEMPLET HOME
PASCAGOULA

Porpoises and ships sweeping by were lagniappe when commercial diver Johnny Templet moved into 600 Beach Blvd. in 1991, a house thought storm proof because of construction that included a berm. "My friends kid me, 'So where's your hurricane-proof house?' I tell them it withstood the hurricane, but not the dad-gum tsunami."

PHOTOGRAPH COURTESY OF CHERYL TEMPLET-FAULK

PHOTOGRAPH: JOHN FITZHUGH

WALKER HOME
OCEAN SPRINGS

Intrigued by its history, Jan Walker, owner of Five Seasons market, bought the 1884 cottage six years ago. Built in New Orleans as the Alabama welcome center for the Cotton & Industrial Centennial Exposition and afterward moved to 243 Front Beach: "I'm doing a restoration, not repairs, to bring it back to its formal glory."

PHOTOGRAPH COURTESY OF JAN WALKER

PHOTOGRAPH: RAY L. BELLANDE

MANY OAKS
OCEAN SPRINGS

The Spanish-moss covered oaks complemented five cottages and the 1918 "Big House" built by a New Orleans stevedore that Mary Jensen bought in 1972. Katrina claimed the moss, three cottages and parts of the house in which they survived. The retired insurance agent and husband David are living in the livable part of the house.

PHOTOGRAPH: RAY L. BELLANDE

PHOTOGRAPH: JOHN FITZHUGH

OTHER AREAS

FORT MASSACHUSETTS
SHIP ISLAND
GULF ISLAND
NATIONAL SEASHORE

U.S. Secretary of War Jefferson Davis realized Ship Island's importance to New Orleans' defense, and that is why today there is a fort. Construction began on Fort Massachusetts in 1859, the Civil War came before it was finished and Davis left Washington to lead the Confederacy. Another part of the fort was later used as a quarantine station for ship passengers suspected of disease. Camille put a cut through the island, and Katrina widened it 2 miles. The old fort survived.

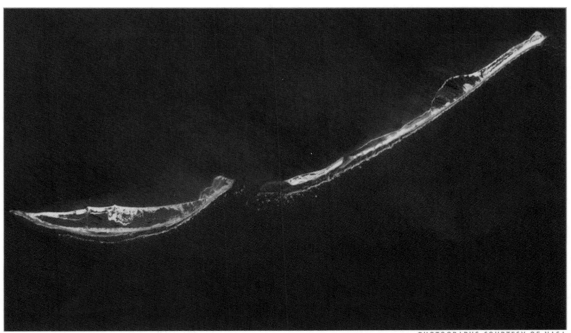

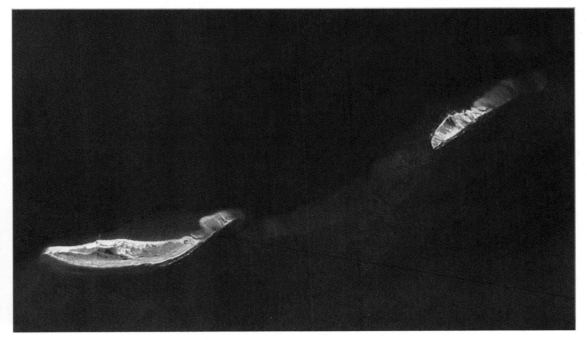

PHOTOGRAPHS COURTESY OF PHYLLIS SHOEMAKE

PECAN HOUSE
MCHENRY

South Mississippians, and people throughout the world, have enjoyed the sweet Southern delicacies offered at the Pecan House in McHenry. These confections, including fudge, pralines and pies, are from the secret recipes of Barbara Overstreet, the former owner. Her daughter, Phyllis Shoemake, now owns the business on U.S. 49.

Overstreet started the Pecan House in 1983, building it with wood used from the vats of an old Wiggins pickle factory. Katrina claimed the wooden walls. "It just made me heartsick. Those walls were special to us, especially because my brother helped build it and he's gone now," Shoemake said. "My whole family had to come and see it because at some point in their lives they have worked here." The shop has reopened.

SAWMILL FAMILY RESTAURANT WIGGINS

A popular country restaurant, the Sawmill Family Restaurant in Wiggins, survived Katrina, but didn't weather one of its tornadoes very well. "The insurance company determined it was a tornado. We've replaced everything," said owner Elaine Beckham. "It took most of the front porch. We've rebuilt or replaced some walls, replaced flooring, the roof and the ceilings." If you were worried about Luther, a large wooden alligator that greeted guests in the front area, Beckham says he came through fine. The Sawmill was built in 1983 or '84 and Beckham purchased it in 1998. The building was once a Christian bookstore and a clothing store.

PHOTOGRAPH: JESSICA POTTS

PHOTOGRAPH COURTESY OF SAWMILL RESTAURANT

FLINT CREEK CABIN
WIGGINS

The rustic interiors and simple furnishings of the A-frame cabins in Flint Creek Water Park in Stone County are a rural getaway for Coast residents. Katrina wasn't so kind to Cabin 15 at Flint Creek Water Park, but the damage gives a peek into the piney woods setting that lures park regulars.

PHOTOGRAPHS COURTESY OF PAT HARRISON WATERWAY DISTRICT

COACH CEDAR CREEK FARMS
AGRICOLA

While in college, Doug "Coach" Byrd and wife Barbara K opened a nursery and maintained it after he became a Pascagoula teacher. Byrd left teaching and now operates in a county with more than 50 nurseries. The Byrds took the greenhouse coverings off in preparation for Katrina but lost 20 greenhouses anyway.

PHOTOGRAPHS COURTESY OF COACH'S NURSERY

PINECOTE PAVILION
PICAYUNE

Small but visually powerful Pinecote snared the nation's highest award from the American Institute of Architects. The pavilion is nestled in Picayune at Crosby Arboretum, a native plant conservatory of the Mississippi State University Extension Service. The arboretum opened in 1978, and the pavilion in 1986. It was designed by architects Fay Jones, a student of Frank Lloyd Wright, and Maurice Jennings. The family of L.O. Crosby Jr., lumberman who made his fortune from the native forests of Pearl River County and elsewhere, established Crosby as a living memorial to him.

PHOTOGRAPH: JAMES EDWARD BATES

PHOTOGRAPHS COURTESY OF MSU EXTENSION SERVICE

July 17, 2001

August 31, 2005

PHOTOGRAPHS COURTESY OF USGS

THE CHANDELEUR ISLANDS

The archipelago of barrier islands that lies 30 miles south of Biloxi is made from wave-deposited sand and silt delivered from the Mississippi River. Called the Chandeleur Islands, they have long been hallowed fishing grounds and Mother Nature's coastal defense against storms, but Katrina submerged the islands, stripped sand from the beaches and eroded much of the marsh. Little is recognizable from the chain of islands already buffeted by four hurricanes in the 21st century.

INDEX

BILOXI BEACH AMUSEMENT
PARK DINOSAUR

The dinosaur at Biloxi
Beach Amusement Park
had become a symbol
of survival after making
it through Hurricane
Camille. It was felled by
Hurricane Katrina. In the
background, a rainstorm
from Hurricane Rita pours
into the Mississippi Sound
on Thursday, Sept. 22,
2005, three weeks after
Katrina hit the area.

PHOTOGRAPH: JOHN FITZHUGH

GULFPORT BEACH

Rebecca Dearmon of Gulfport walks in February, 2006, amid the debris on the beach from Hurricane Katrina exposed by low tide in Gulfport. "You wonder how something so beautiful could create so much destruction," she said.

PHOTOGRAPH: JOHN FITZHUGH

Back Cover Photographs

A SIGN OF PROGRESS
GULFPORT

The poignant signs on 916 East Blvd., in Gulfport say it all. Jim and Donna Parks, who moved to the Mississippi Coast from Utah in 1961, have put into words the loss, frustrations and hopes of more than 65,000 others whose homes were destroyed by Katrina. The Parkses have faced looters, frustrating dealings with governmental agencies, and the wonders of the thousands of selfless people who have poured to the Coast to help recover and rebuild. In a March letter to the *Sun Herald*, the retired couple commented, "We want to begin building our new home in May, but this place looks like Hiroshima the day after the bomb."

PHOTOGRAPHS: DAVID PURDY